Dust from the Master's Feet

J. H. Osborne

TABLE OF CONTENTS

Chapters

INTRODUCTION

The disciples who followed their Master the closest, such as Peter, James, and John, talked with Him along the way, asked Him questions, and tried to absorb His teaching. For three and a half years, they trudged after Him over the dusty trails throughout Galilee, Samaria, and Judea, eager to hear what He had to say and marvel over the amazing things He could do. Jesus taught kingdom precepts with parables; the crowds heard the parables, but the ones closest to Him heard their meaning and received greater understanding. Time spent in His proximity forged a lifetime bond. At the end of each day, the disciples who followed Him the closest were covered with a sprinkling of dust from the Master's feet.

I would not presume the words of this book to be the entire counsel of God, but rather the humble effort of one, who if not always the closest, has yet been striving to follow the Master for some fifty-five years.

This book is my offering of some common yet precious dust from the Master's feet. I pray that the insights you find will quicken your spirit and compel you to follow your Master more closely. At the end of your day, may it be said you were covered with dust from the Master's feet.

ACKNOWLEDGEMENTS

My deepest appreciation to my wife, Judy, who, next to the Lord, is my most cherished friend. Thank you, sweetheart, for your unwavering love and loyalty to me during our thirty-eight-year pastorate.

I am grateful to my children for the sacrifice they have made in time spent with Dad, which enabled my study time reflected in this book.

A special thanks to my daughter Kelly, and her husband, Ben. What on earth would I do without you two by my side? Your support and love have been for me the shadow of a rock in a weary land. Thank you for two beautiful grandchildren, Holly and Joe. You guys are the greatest.

To all the men and ministries who have so unreservedly poured themselves into my life; accept my sincerest gratitude.

To the First Bible Church, my church family, who have been a source of inspiration and the sounding board for every sermon, both the bitter and the sweet. Thank you for your kindness and understanding.

A owe a special debt of gratitude to my editor, Patricia Bollmann. Thank you for lending yourself so unreservedly to this project. I know that without you and your God-given talent this effort would have languished in the backwaters of good intentions.

Most important, I thank my God for His indescribable gift of the Holy Ghost and the faithful guidance, love, and grace He has given me all the days of my life.

Chapter 1

Divine Disappointment

Now let me sing to my Well-beloved a song of my Beloved regarding His vineyard: "My Well-beloved has a vineyard on a very fruitful hill. He dug it up and cleared out its stones, and planted it with the choicest vine. He built a tower in its midst, and also made a winepress in it. So He expected it to bring forth good grapes, but it brought forth wild grapes. And now, O inhabitants of Jerusalem and men of Judah, judge, please, between Me and My vineyard. What more could have been done to My vineyard that I have not done in it? Why then, when I expected it to bring forth good grapes, did it bring forth wild grapes?" (Isaiah 5:1-4, NKJV).

The Old Testament narratives about Israel give us an advantage; we see not only her victories, but also her faults and failures. We note God's response and reaction to both her obedience to God and her transgressions. All of this was recorded as an admonition to us so we might learn about God's goodness and God's severity.

Paul explained God's reaction to sin in I Corinthians 10:5-11: "With many of them [the Jews] God was not well pleased: for they were overthrown in the wilderness. Now these things were our examples, to the intent we should not lust after evil things, as they lusted." He went on to list Israel's sins in the wilderness: idolatry, fornication, and tempting God with their murmuring. When Israel sinned, God dealt with them severely.

Paul also explained that Israel's failings opened the door of salvation to Gentile Christians. These Christians are "Jews" because of the work Christ Jesus has done in their hearts. Instead of outward, fleshly circumcision, He has "circumcised" their hearts in the Spirit. (See Romans 2:28-29.) Instead of being the earthly descendants of Abraham, the "sand which is upon the sea shore," those in the church are the spiritual descendants of Abraham, "the stars of the heaven." (See Genesis 22:17.)

If we as Christians continue to obey and serve Him in holiness, then we will experience His goodness. "Behold therefore the goodness and severity of God: on them which fell, severity; but toward thee, goodness, if thou continue in his goodness" (Romans 11:22).

It has been well said that those who do not learn from history are destined to repeat it. Our nation has not learned much from biblical history. Even

Dust From The Master's Feet

though our nation was founded on basic Christian principles, we as a people have wandered far from our heritage. Thomas Jefferson, in his work, "Notes on the State of Virginia" (1781), wrote, "God who gave us life gave us liberty. And can the liberties of a nation be thought secure when we have removed their only firm basis, a conviction in the minds of the people that these liberties are of the Gift of God? That they are not to be violated but with His wrath? Indeed, I tremble for my country when I reflect that God is just, that his justice cannot sleep forever."

Isaiah 5:1-4 paints a picture of a frustrated and disappointed God. It is an allegory that depicts Israel as a vineyard and God as the Vinedresser who chooses a fertile landscape for His vineyard. He does not trust hirelings to prepare His vineyard; He does the work Himself. He intends to withhold nothing and to give this vineyard every opportunity to fulfill its purpose and design.

The Vinedresser started by preparing the site carefully, for if done well the vineyard would produce year after year. For several months prior to planting, He leveled the soil, fixed drainage problems, and brought any weeds under control. He dug up the stones and carted them off. He didn't want any hindrances as the tender roots pushed deep into the soil to make strong, healthy plants. He did not tolerate anything that did not contribute to the success and fertility of the vines.

When God "planted" Israel in the Promised Land, He removed every idol and false God from the land. He eradicated every object that might preempt Israel's affections for their one true God.

The Vinedresser built a fence that separated and protected His choice vineyard from everything around it. God always distinguishes what belongs to Him from all others. His "hedge" around Israel consisted of laws, ordinances, statutes, observances, civil life, diet, dress, relationships, and government. He wanted Israel to be different, a cut above the mediocre.

The Vinedresser chose the best, most robust vines, ones full of promise for a lush crop. Israel was the best in all the world. God expected them to proliferate until they were as numerous as the sands on the seashore; and in their numerical, commercial, and spiritual growth they would influence and bless the world.

He built a tower in the vineyard. This was not some temporary hut, but a permanent, imposing tower to protect and defend His investment. It could house all the offices and implements, the whole apparatus for the cultivation of the vineyard. He Himself intended to be a strong tower for Israel; when danger approached, they could run to the tower and be safe.

Excited about the first harvest, He built a wine-press. It was not a ramshackle structure that would let the wine spoil or leak out. No, He hewed it out of rock. Workers would tread the grapes in an elevated tank, and when the juice reached the brim it would spill over into the lower storage tanks. The stone tanks would cool the juice and keep it from spoiling.

As the robust vines grew, the Vinedresser kept checking them for the first tender grapes. To His horror, His bumper crop turned out to be wild grapes! Poisonous, invasive, wild grapes. He knew it wouldn't be long before thickets of the wild vines would choke out His choice vines. After all He had done, all He had invested, all of the effort and sweat, this was devastating. It was worse than no grapes; it was a crushing humiliation.

Everything He was and was worth He had put into the vineyard. What more could He have done? What could He have done differently? Where did it all go wrong? He thought, "How could I buy and prepare the most fruitful field, plant only the choicest vines, and end up with wild grapes?" The answer was clear: He had done nothing wrong; He could have done nothing more or differently. Even though He had chosen and prepared the site carefully, something must have been lurking in the soil.

His delight was wiped out by indignation. "Now I will tell you what I am going to do to my vineyard: I will take away its hedge, and it will be destroyed; I will break down its wall, and it will be trampled. I will make it a wasteland, neither pruned nor cultivated, and briers and thorns will grow there. I will command the clouds not to rain on it" (Isaiah 5:5-6, NIV).

Since the vineyard had resisted cultivation, the Vinedresser vowed to destroy the fence and let the wild vines, briars, and thorns take over. This describes how He treated idolatrous, wayward Israel; He took away all the advantages He had provided and left them to themselves. No more would He guard their well-being and their assets. He would ignore them and let them sink into ruin.

In our nation, the strong foundation of Judeo-Christian principles has collapsed. President Obama said during a speech in June 2007, "Whatever we once were, we're no longer a Christian nation. At least not just [a Christian nation]. We are also a Jewish nation, a Muslim nation, and a Buddhist nation, and a Hindu nation, and a nation of nonbelievers."

Later President Obama further explained his remarks to CBN's senior national correspondent, David Brody: "We should acknowledge this and realize . . . we've got to work to translate our reasoning into values that are accessible to every one of our citizens, not just members of our own faith community."

Even though our Declaration of Independence and Constitution are based on Judeo-Christian principles, this does not mean that all the people were or are Christian. It merely means there was a Christian consensus and all our founding documents, laws, moral codes, and institutions are based on Christian principles from the Bible.

Buddhism and Confucianism made China what it is, Shintoism made Japan what it is; Hinduism made India what it is; Islam made the Middle East and North Africa what they are; Communism made thirty nations what they became; and Reformation Christianity made America what it is. And this is the country we choose—and so would millions of others if they could.

This is not to say there is nothing good in other religions. There are good teachings in most religions, and certainly many evil things have been done in the name of Christianity. But don't blame Jesus and His teachings for man's aberrations.

From the early documents and writings of our country—such as the Mayflower Compact (1620), the Fundamental Orders of Connecticut (1638), the Declaration of Independence (1776), and the U.S. Constitution (1787)—we see that our Founding Fathers believed in what is the very essence of our Americanism!

- There is such a thing as Truth, and Truth can be known by man.
- Men are "created" and their rights come from God, their Creator.
- Governments exist to protect these God-given rights.

In the eighteenth century, men such as George Washington, Samuel Adams, John Adams, Patrick Henry, and Benjamin Franklin made profound statements like the following:

- "The rights of the colonists as Christians may be best understood by reading and carefully studying the institutes of the great Law Giver which are to be found clearly written and promulgated in the New Testament."
- "The propitious smiles of heaven cannot be expected on a nation that disregards the eternal rules of order and right, which heaven itself has ordained."
- The first and almost the only Book deserving of universal attention is the Bible."

In 1892, the U.S. Supreme Court, after citing eighty-seven precedents, decided that "our laws and our institutions must necessarily be based upon and embody the teachings of the Redeemer of Mankind. It is impossible that it should be otherwise: and in this sense and to this extent our civilization and our institutions are emphatically Christian."

A joint congressional resolution of October 4, 1983, states, "The Word of God has made a unique contribution in shaping the United States as a distinctive and blessed nation of people. Whereas Biblical teachings inspired concepts of civil government that are contained in our Declaration of

Independence and the Constitution of The United States . . . Whereas that renewing our knowledge of, and faith in God through Holy Scriptures can strengthen us as a nation and a people. Now therefore be it resolved . . . that the President is authorized and requested to designate 1983 as a national 'Year of the Bible' in recognition of both the formative influence the Bible has been for our nation, and our national need to study and apply the teachings of the Holy Scriptures."

All of this cultivating of the soil of a new nation and planting of godly seed has not produced a nation of people who love God and obey His Word. Instead, two centuries after this country's inception, we are a spiritually apathetic society that hardly gave a murmur of protest when, in 1962, our liberal Supreme Court abolished prayer in public schools and the next year abolished Bible reading in the schools. Throughout the intervening years, we as a nation have been conditioned to accept these paradigmatic shifts. Since 1962 we saw a startlingly great rise in teenage pregnancies (up 556 percent) and venereal disease (up 226 percent). Family divorce, which had declined for fifteen years prior to 1962, has tripled each year since. S.A.T. scores, previously stable, have declined remarkably. The high principles that made America have eroded away.

Old Foes with New Faces

"The vineyard of the LORD Almighty is the house of Israel, and the men of Judah are the garden of his delight. And he looked for justice, but saw bloodshed; for righteousness, but heard cries of distress. Woe to you who add house to house and join field to field till no space is left and you live alone in the land. The LORD Almighty has declared in my hearing: 'Surely the great houses will become desolate, the fine mansions left without occupants' " (Isaiah 5:7-9).

In 2009 there was an insatiable appetite for land-grabbing and house-building. Construction increased beyond measure. Homes sprang up until it seemed there was nowhere else to build.

Suddenly, the housing market crashed. There were now too many houses and too few occupants. Expensive, spacious homes sat empty and desolate. For sale signs sprang up everywhere, but there was no market for the houses.

"Woe to those who rise early in the morning to run after their drinks, who stay up late at night till they are inflamed with wine" (Isaiah 5:11, NIV). The wild grapes of alcohol flourish. Lives and families are wrecked, jobs are lost, and innocent people are killed by drunk drivers.

"They have harps and lyres at their banquets, tambourines and flutes and wine, but they have no regard for the deeds of the LORD, no respect for the work of his hands" (Isaiah 5:12, NIV). The wild grapes of gluttony, rap, and rock music—alternative, punk, hardcore, metal, and crossover to name a few—try to choke out the good grapes of moderation and music that glorifies God.

"Therefore my people are gone into captivity, because they have no knowledge: and their honourable men are famished, and their multitude dried up with thirst" (Isaiah 5:13). The wild grapes of deceptive, self-serving leaders try to drown out the voices of faithful, upright, honorable, leaders. In this leadership vacuum, people wander like sheep without a shepherd, lost and vulnerable.

In her infancy our nation enjoyed the favor and blessings of God as long as she honored His Word in her government, in her schools, and in the citizens' lives. But two centuries later this has all changed. Wild grapes are taking over the vineyard and now seem to produce more fruit than the good vines. Our nation is a divine disappointment. Sadly, the just desserts of rampant national wickedness will reap, instead of blessings and favor, the judgments and wrath of God.

But even after centuries of divine disappointment in Israel, God's wrath turned to regret. He would rather bestow blessing than judgment, favor than disgrace. He did not vent His wrath indefinitely. He offered to forgive Israel if she would commit to restoring relationship with Him and renew her covenant with Him. "If my people, which are called by my name, shall humble themselves, and pray, and seek my face, and turn from their wicked ways: then will I hear from heaven, and will forgive their sin, and will heal their land" (II Chronicles 7:14).

In Isaiah 27 there is a song of the Lord's restoration of His vineyard:

> *Sing about a fruitful vineyard;*
> *I, the Lord, watch over it,*
> *I water it continually.*
> *I guard it day and night*
> *So that no one may harm it.*
> *I am not angry.*
> *If only there were briers and thorns*
> *confronting me!*
> *I would march against them in battle;*
> *I would set them all on fire.*
> *Or else let them come to me for refuge;*
> *let them make peace with me . . .*
> *In days to come Jacob will take root,*
> *Israel will bud and blossom*
> *And fill all the world with fruit*
> *(Isaiah 27:3-6, NIV).*

Just as there was a remedy for Israel's transgressions and plight, there is a remedy for our own faults and sins. There is also hope for our nation if we will ask God's forgiveness and once again honor Him by renewing our commitments to love Him and obey His precepts.

Chapter 2

Fighting for the Increase

*A*nd *the children of Israel did evil in the sight of the* LORD: *and the* LORD *delivered them into the hand of Midian seven years. And the hand of Midian prevailed against Israel: and because of the Midianites the children of Israel made them the dens which are in the mountains, and caves, and strong holds. And so it was, when Israel had sown, that the Midianites came up, and the Amalekites, and the children of the east, even they came up against them; and they encamped against them, and destroyed the increase of the earth, till thou come unto Gaza, and left no sustenance for Israel, neither sheep, nor ox, nor ass. For they came up with their cattle and their tents, and they came as grasshoppers for multitude; for both they and their camels were without number: and they entered into the land to destroy it. And Israel was greatly impoverished because of the*

Midianites; and the children of Israel cried unto the LORD *(Judges 6:1-6).*

The Midianites inhabited the region east of the Gulf of Aquaba, in the northwest territory of the Arabian Peninsula. Because their land was inhospitable, many of them became nomads, herders of sheep and goats, while others were slave traders or caravaneers. But many made their living by raiding other people's territories.

At the time of the judges the Midianites had no organized military, only rugged tribesmen with slings, bows, and javelins. They didn't really need a trained army because raids into their own territory were rare. Their land was a remote, hostile environment with nothing anyone else would want. If they ever met a formidable military foe, they probably would have fled from them or at least given them a wide berth.

The Midianites had advantages, though, such as the domesticated camel. Camels were uniquely suited for the sparse, scruffy countryside. The nomads depended on them for milk, meat, wool, and transportation. These ungainly, cantankerous beasts could carry quarter-ton loads, weather sand storms, and adjust easily to extreme temperature fluctuations common to a desert. Some rode their camels when on a raid; their size alone intimidated the Jewish farmers who ran for the hills and caves. Then the raiders loaded their camels with ill-gotten booty and headed homeward, driving the lowing cattle and bleating sheep.

The Midianites did not get along with very many of their neighbors, the Edomites, Moabites, and Ammonites. But most of their hatred and contempt was for Israel. Maybe their dislike stemmed from jealousy because they envied Israel's fertile land and coveted her abundant crops and prolific herds. Israel had everything; in comparison, the nomads had nothing.

It had been only forty years since Deborah and Barak's victory over Sisera, but as soon as the threat was removed Israel reverted back to their evil, idolatrous ways. Therefore, the Lord permitted Midian's two tribal kings, Zebah and Zalmunna, to help themselves to Israel's bounty. But they didn't work alone. As they often did, the two kings amassed an innumerable horde by allying with the Amalekites and other eastern peoples. The allies defeated Israel not by strategic conflict or siege, but by waiting until Israel's harvests were ready and swarming out of the desert like a mighty locust plague stripping the land of grain, vegetables, fruit, and livestock. Then they loaded the camels with huge packs of produce and herded the livestock back to their tents. They could live sumptuously on the spoil until the next harvest.

Midian's strategy intrigues me. They seized the Israelites' increase, but did not destroy their ability and means to produce more. The enemy federation left Israel's houses, barns, and farm implements virtually untouched. They did not molest the people; they didn't even take prisoners. No, their objective was getting their greedy hands on the *increase*.

As long as Israel feared God and remained true to His precepts, they prospered and defeated their enemies. But in this period of the Judges, they gained increase every year but God allowed their enemies to snatch it away. The raiders would

- Leave the donkey but take her colt;
- Leave the ox but take her calf;
- Leave the ewe but take her lambs;
- Leave the goat but take her kids;
- Leave the orchard but take its fruit;
- Leave the vines but take the grapes;
- Leave the winepress but take the wine;
- Leave the stalks but take the ears;
- Leave the cupboards but take the flour and meal;
- Leave the kneading trough but take the bread;
- Leave the bees but take the honey;
- Leave the seed for next year's crops but steal this year's harvest.

This vicious cycle went on for seven years. Midian and her allies kept running off with their bounty until Israel became impoverished. They never knew from what direction or at what time the hordes would descend: would it be while they were stacking the sheaves, treading the grapes, birthing the young animals, shearing the sheep, gathering the figs and pomegranates, or crushing the olives? They were virtual captives in their own land, doing all the work but gaining no wealth, suffering want from harvest to harvest. It seemed that their enemies were too numerous, too strong, too violent, and too crafty. Instead of uniting and fighting, they would abandon their fields and herds and run for their lives. It was not that the increase was never there; it was just that they were not willing to stay and fight to keep it.

I think it is safe to say that the twenty-first century strategy of Satan has not changed. His goal is the same—to devour your increase.

Increase is what God adds to your life after you've put in the time and effort to achieve His will. Paul said, "I planted, Apollos watered, but God gave the increase. So then neither he who plants is anything, nor he who waters, but God who gives the increase" (I Corinthians 3:6-7, NKJV). God wants to increase our spiritual stature, our borders, our influence, and our churches; in short, give us "more and more" (Psalm 115:14).

It seems there is no end to His blessings. But what good does all the bounty do if we don't hold on to it? It makes little sense to let the increase be snatched from our grasp, to let our enemy constantly shove us back down to ground zero. It would be like a weary, footsore donkey thinking he might be getting somewhere, not realizing he is hitched to a mill by a pole and trudging in endless circles.

Increase can come both individually and corporately. How can you as an individual experience increase?

- Fearing the Lord and being changed into His likeness
- Producing spiritual fruit and righteousness
- Practicing generosity
- Growing in wisdom and knowledge
- Increasing in faith
- Prospering in spiritual as well as physical health
- Adding virtue, temperance, patience, and godliness
- Even abounding in Christ's suffering so He can abound in comforting you.

How can a church experience increase?

- "Publish" the good news everywhere
- Add souls to the church
- Cultivate love for one another, edify one another, prefer one another
- Strive for unity in deed and thought—stick together
- Abound in brotherly kindness and forbearance

- Do good works motivated by love for God and others
- Place ever-increasing value on the Word of God.

A church "maketh increase of the body unto the edifying of itself in love" (Ephesians 4:16). "And the Lord make you to increase and abound in love one toward another, and toward all men . . . to the end he may stablish your hearts unblameable in holiness before God" (I Thessalonians 3:12-13). Jesus said, "If ye continue in my word, then are ye my disciples indeed" (John 8:31). Jesus said, "By this shall all men know that ye are my disciples, if ye have love one to another."

There is a flipside of an individual's increase. Those who disregard God's bounty, are careless with it, misuse it, horde it to themselves without giving thanks, or think they can get away with doing wrong, are in danger of having their good fortune snatched away. "The heaven shall reveal his iniquity; and . . . The increase of his house shall depart, and his goods shall flow away in the day of [God's] wrath" (Job 20:27-28). Keeping and enjoying our increase, whether individual or corporate, requires diligence, obedience to God's commands, submission to His will, and a willingness to fight for what we have gained lest an enemy seize it.

The flipside of a church's increase is factions, cliques, rivalry, emulation, jealousy, self-importance, power-grabbing—anything that would destroy unity and love. Those who do not value the written Word of God or what comes across the pulpit become careless and spiritually lethargic. They forget to watch for the enemy, and some wander away from the corporate body. All of these and more can leave us vulnerable to an enemy raid.

Israel finally did the right thing: they cried unto God for help. Instead of turning His back on them as they had done to Him, God heard their pleas and called Gideon to deliver them from the Midianite federation. On purpose, God limited Israel's army so they would know their deliverance came from Him. He went before Israel and added His strength to the battle.

In the middle of the night the enemy jerked awake when they heard the ear-splitting surround sound of three hundred trumpets and saw lights blazing from every side. They panicked, got confused, went for each other's throats, then realized the Israelites were descending on them to wipe them out if they didn't do something. They turned and fled for their lives, Gideon and his men at their heels, dispatching the enemy on every side. The battle ended when Gideon slew the two tribal kings, Zeba and Zalmunna. This year, the Israelites would keep their increase!

It is one thing to produce increase, but it's another thing to hold on to it. How can you fight to keep your increase, the fruit of all your efforts?

Watch out for the enemy at harvest time and remember you have to resist and fight to keep what you've gained. The harvest is yours; you worked for it. It's your possession and your estate.

- You must resist the enemy and defend what you have.
- Encourage others to resist and help them. Stand together.
- Realize that the enemy may look formidable and ferocious, but God is on your side; who can be against you?
- You are vulnerable only if you choose to be; if you do right, trust in God, and stand with the group, the enemy is vulnerable, not you.
- Protect the young and weak ones. Don't let them wander away on their own. Encourage them and let them lean on your spiritual strength.
- Teach them by instruction and example how to recognize the enemy and his intent and how to defend what they have.
- Watch out for each other and warn each other in love when you see an oncoming threat.
- Pick each other up if one trips or falls.
- Above all, don't hesitate to fight for what you've gained. Don't give the devil any ground, not even a toehold.

You can keep all of your increase if you're willing to fight for it.

Chapter 3

A Man and His Lamb

The story of a man and his lamb goes like this:

And the LORD sent Nathan unto David. And he came unto him, and said unto him, There were two men in one city; the one rich, and the other poor. The rich man had exceeding many flocks and herds: but the poor man had nothing, save one little ewe lamb, which he had bought and nourished up: and it grew up together with him, and with his children; it did eat of his own meat, and drank of his own cup, and lay in his bosom, and was unto him as a daughter. And there came a traveler unto the rich man, and he spared to take of his own flock and of his own herd, to dress for the wayfaring man that was come unto him; but took the poor man's lamb, and dressed it for the man that was come to him (II Samuel 12:1-4).

The prophet Nathan was not looking forward to his audience with the king. He was going at God's behest, but the mission was distasteful and intimidating. And potentially dangerous. Kings had been known to have bearers of bad news executed on the spot.

The matter was serious. Nathan had been sent to pronounce judgment on King David for taking Uriah's wife, the beautiful Bathsheba, and for ordering his commanding officer to make sure Uriah was killed in battle. To further twist the knife, David sent Uriah himself to deliver the fateful, sealed message. David thought his misdeed would be safely buried along with the fallen soldier.

Even though Nathan had probably not known David in his youth, he was aware he was not dealing with the David of bygone days. David the shepherd boy had been a naïve harp player and a psalmist who was sensitive to God's presence and anointed by Samuel. He had nurtured and protected his flock, fighting off beasts that would devour his lambs. He had loved the Lord with a pure, fierce love that was the impetus for his volunteering to face the Philistine giant who dared to defy Yahweh.

But the David that Nathan knew was not the same man as David the shepherd boy. Many precious things were missing. His naïveté had been replaced with sophistication, his tenderness with callousness. He was accustomed to a rich, lavish lifestyle and having his every whim gratified. Successfully conquering Israel's enemies had left him with too much time on his hands and he turned to indulging his greed and lust, vices he had not known were in him. Lies replaced truth and overshadowed all better judgment. Now justice meant how the outcome could benefit his own interests, not those of his loyal subjects. His position as king became a license to satisfy his own appetites with little thought for the price or consequences.

The change had not happened in the early years of his reign. Soon after David had ascended to the throne he brought the sacred ark to Jerusalem with dancing and sacrifices, burnt offerings and peace offerings. But the ark had no permanent dwelling; it was still in a tent. David had summoned Nathan and talked of his desire to build a magnificent house for God. Nathan could see the passion and love for his God in the king's eyes. Although David's dream was not fulfilled until after he died, he spent countless energy and wealth amassing costly materials for the future house of God.

David had once had a tender heart. His compassion and kindness led him to inquire if any of his friend Jonathan's heirs had survived the trauma of the time of King Saul's death. He wanted to honor his friendship with Jonathan by taking care of his descendents for the rest of their lives.

But today when Nathan faced the king, he knew he would be looking into the cold, calculating eyes of another man, a man who was a stranger to the

David of the past. In what way could he approach the king that would, instead of fomenting his wrath against a prophet, appeal to the kernel of kindness that surely was still in there somewhere?

He needed a case, a scenario to trigger the king's righteous judgment and open his eyes to error. This case had to have emotional relevance to King David and arouse his sympathies. Regardless of the jewel-encrusted crown on his head and the royal robes on his person, a vestige of the shepherd boy still had to be inside. And what could strum the tender heart-strings of a shepherd more than a story of a man and his lamb?

Nathan carefully crafted a story that would have great significance for David even if it would mean little to any other king. This story would touch David's heart because it was inspired of God.

When it came time for his audience with the king, Nathan began his story.

A rich man and a poor man were citizens of the same city. However, the only things they had in common were that they spoke the same language and abided by the same laws. Economically they were on the opposite ends of the spectrum so they lived in totally different worlds.

The rich man's life was replete with opulence and vanity. He dined on gourmet food and lived in a grand mansion. He enjoyed the best of the city's resources, having outmaneuvered and outdone all his competitors. He had name recognition, popularity, prestige, and favor. His barns were bursting with produce and his pastures teeming with flocks and herds.

In contrast, the poor man's life was one of insufficiency and want. He and his family eked out a hard-scrabble existence on the wrong side of the tracks. They were used to doing without most of what the city had to offer. The poor man had no flocks or herds, no security, prestige, social standing, or name. More often than not, he and his family went to bed hungry.

Let us pause to point out that Nathan's story had several layers of meaning; "a man and his lamb" was part of an ever-flowing theme wending its way through the Scriptures as they testified of Him (the Lamb) (John 5:39).

- As Abraham and his son Isaac climbed the mountain to offer a sacrifice, Isaac asked why they weren't bringing along a lamb. Abraham replied, "My son, God will provide himself a lamb."
- At the institution of the first Passover, Moses instructed the people that every man needed a lamb. The Israelites should "keep [the lamb] up" for four days. (See Exodus 12:6.) David Guzik comments on the meaning of "keep it up": the lamb was to live with the family four days so they would cherish it. They were to bond with it so the lamb's life's blood was

precious to them and they would attach value to the sacrifice.

- Isaiah foretold a Lamb who would bear the iniquities of us all and be brought as a lamb to the slaughter.
- John the Baptist saw Jesus coming toward him and declared, "Behold the Lamb of God, which taketh away the sin of the world."
- The climax of this theme is in the Revelation of Jesus Christ, in which the Lamb springs forth in all His power, glory, and majesty. He is the slain Lamb who is worthy of all worship because He has overcome by His saving blood and removed the curse from mankind and the earth. He alone is worthy to open the seal. The Lamb receives his bride at the marriage supper. The Lamb is the light of the temple.

Scripture lifts its voice like a trumpeter playing one refrain: Jesus Christ, the great Lamb of God!

John the Revelator said this Lamb was "slain from the foundation of the world" (Revelation 13:8). "Foundation" means "conception," or when the world and the cosmos were created and placed in an orderly arrangement. From the conception of the cosmos, God envisioned a slain Lamb whose blood would redeem those who believe on Him. The Lamb's kingdom was to last forever, but man, His crowning creation, would not survive unless he was reunited with his Lamb.

At the time of the prophet Nathan's audience with the king, the Hebrew Scriptures probably consisted of the Torah, or the five Books of Moses. Nathan was aware of the theme of the Lamb found in the Torah. Thus his story for King David was a stroke of genius. Nathan hinted at the scriptural theme of the Lamb while simultaneously appealing to David's memory of what he once was. David had been both a poor man and a rich man. He had once experienced a close relationship with his flocks, but he had buried these memories beneath many layers of fleeing for his life, fighting off foes, conquering nations, and having underlings obey his every word and satisfy his every desire. His conscience was seared by the heat of unrepented sin and unworthy judgments.

The prophet's narrative continued.

The poor man had only one tangible asset: his chosen ewe lamb. Their fellowship and communion was a ray of light in a dark and gloomy world. He nurtured his lamb, furnishing her with the same food and care he gave to his family. If the family ate, the lamb ate. Whatever the family drank, the lamb drank. The man shared his own cup with the lamb. He even invited the lamb into his bed.

The lamb was like one of the kids and integrated into the family's home life. In fact, the man thought of her as a daughter. The man's children loved the lamb and they grew up together. They played with the lamb and lavished affection on her.

One could not separate the lamb from the man; it was who he was and what he was. The man's heart was knit with the lamb's; his heartstrings were wound tightly around her. He loved his lamb with an enduring love. The man and his lamb were inseparable; everywhere he went he could hear her little hooves tapping in his wake.

The poor man had the one thing King David lacked; he had a relationship with his lamb. David had thousands of lambs and flocks on every hill, but something had broken the bond between this man and his lamb. His lamb no longer ate at his table, drank from his cup, or slept on his bed. David was estranged from his lamb. Instead of a man and his lamb, David's life had become a man and his herds, a man and his armies, a man and his kingdom, his palaces, his wives, his money, his prestige, his ego, his power.

It is easy for a man to kill a lamb when he has no feelings for it, no relationship with it, no love for it. There is no passion or connection, no affection or bond. He does not share the lamb with his children or allow it to eat at his table or drink from his cup. He wouldn't dream of letting the lamb sleep on his bed. It would be simple and painless to kill an unchosen lamb; it was just a lamb—not *his* lamb.

Though the rich man and the poor man lived poles apart, there came a day when their lives overlapped. An unexpected guest showed up on the rich man's doorstep and common hospitality at its least dictated that he provide a meal, but he didn't care to sacrifice any of his own lambs; it was time to take them to market and he didn't want to lose a penny. He thought of the poor man's lamb. He had seen it trotting behind the man at the farmer's market. The rich man had no connection to it. Killing it would neither stab his heart nor injure his pocket-book. He ordered a servant to seize the poor man's lamb—he didn't care how much force he had to use. The servant took the lamb, slit its throat, skinned it, butchered it, and gave it to the cook. The rich man's guest would soon enjoy a savory lamb stew.

My grandfather was a farmer in Kentucky. He raised seven children on that farm. For him, farming was not a hobby or a pastime; it was serious business—life or death, success or failure. He never got attached to the farm animals. They were all a means to an end. He raised hogs, beef cattle, milk cows, chickens, beagles, foxhounds, coonhounds, and cats. The only animals who received names were the dogs—the farm animals remained nameless.

The thought of his farm animals did not pull at Granddad's heartstrings. His animals didn't evoke affection or arouse a desire to form a connection. If the cow stopped giving milk, it was the stock-yards. The day the chicken stopped laying eggs, it landed in the skillet. Any dog that wouldn't obey or hunt got traded to the first man who came along. If a cat got too lazy to control the mice popula-tion, Granddad got a large sack, loaded it with a good-sized rock, scooped the cat into it, and headed to the pond. He refused to feed an animal or call the vet for that which did not fulfill its purpose or supply his need.

People who treat the Lamb like my grandfather treated his farm animals, those who stop producing, fail to meet His expectations, stop giving to His needs, don't come when He calls, or do as He asks, will not be permitted to eat at His table, drink from His cup, or sleep in His bosom. The problem is that people seldom bond with the Lamb, and the detachment makes it so easy to walk away from Him.

Nathan's story accomplished its purpose. David leaped to his feet, wrath flashing from his eyes like lightning. He thundered, "As surely as the LORD lives, the man who did this deserves to die! He must pay for that lamb four times over, because he did such a thing and had no pity" (II Samuel 12:5, NIV).

Nathan thundered back, "You are the man!" As the words pierced the king's soul, his wrath fizzled out. The prophet delivered the Lord's message that He had given David every possible gift and advantage and yet he had "struck down Uriah the Hittite with the sword and [taken] his wife" for his own (II Samuel 12:9, NIV). Nathan predicted that calamity would plague David's house. Smitten with remorse, David mourned, "I have sinned against the Lord." He repented, but he and his family suffered the consequences of sin for many years.

David's verdict against the man who killed the lamb was twofold: (1) restore four lambs for the one he killed; (2) the man himself must die. One half of his sentence was carried out as one by one four of his sons died by various means: Bathsheba's son, Ammon, Absalom, and Adonijah. As for the other half of the verdict, a part of David died that day as the dark shadow of his guilt and shame loomed over his dying soul. Psalm 51 was a death rattle in the throat of a man separated from his God. As he sought mercy and restoration with his great Lamb, David pleaded

- have mercy on me;
- wash me;
- make me;
- create in me;
- cast me not away;
- restore unto me;
- deliver me.

This story is not about a man and his church or his congregation. It is not about a man and his recognition or reputation in the world. It's not about a man and his profession or his talent or giftedness. When life is distilled down to its most basic components, it's about a man and his Lamb.

Nothing else matters if a man loses his bond with his Lamb. If he becomes detached, he forfeits any relationship he may have had with the Lamb. He loses his passion and love for the Lamb until it's easy to fall away and crucify Him afresh. The Lamb no longer drinks from his cup, eats from his table, or sleeps in his bosom. There is no intimacy; the Lamb is no longer his prized possession.

When we have a genuine bond with the Lamb of God, He does not have to perform in order to earn our love and loyalty. He doesn't have to lavish riches and recognition and resources on us. We are content just to have the Lamb as a constant and cherished companion. We realize the inestimable value of the Lamb's shed blood being applied to our lives and hearts, and it makes us love Him even more. Our heartstrings are wound tightly around our Lamb. He is worthy of worship and we desire to do His bidding. Above anything else, we don't want to lose our close connection with Him.

Nothing is as important as the close, loving relationship between a man and his Lamb. My prayer is that you will make sure your connection with your Lamb is affectionate, passionate, and unbreakable. That you cherish Him and commune with Him until it becomes the catalyst for your family's bond with the Lamb.

Chapter 4

My Father Is a Husbandman

*A*nd the remnant that is escaped of the house of
Judah shall yet again take root downward, and
bear fruit upward (II Kings 19:30).

I am the true vine, and my Father is the
husbandman. Every branch in me that beareth not
fruit he taketh away: and every branch that beareth
fruit, he purgeth it, that it may bring forth more
fruit. Now ye are clean through the word which I
have spoken unto you. Abide in me, and I in you. As
the branch cannot bear fruit of itself, except it abide
in the vine; no more can ye, except ye abide in me.
I am the vine, ye are the branches: He that abideth
in me, and I in him, the same bringeth forth much
fruit: for without me ye can do nothing. If a man
abide not in me, he is cast forth as a branch, and is
withered; and men gather them, and cast them into
the fire, and they are burned. If ye abide in me, and
my words abide in you, ye shall ask what ye will,

and it shall be done unto you. Herein is my Father glorified, that ye bear much fruit; so shall ye be my disciples (John 15:1-8).

God is a Spirit but He is often described in anthropomorphic terms, which ascribe to Him human shapes or traits. For example, many writers of Scripture used terms such as hand or arm or eyes or heart of God. Some depict God as walking or riding, coming down or moving, fighting or protecting. He experiences many of the same feelings we experience: jealousy or delight, sorrow or joy, love or hate. In our human condition we relate to these terms and thereby come to know and understand more about our God.

Besides human shapes or traits or feelings, God is often described in terms of occupation: master-builder, captain of salvation, advocate, author. This is because we understand someone better when we know what kind of labor occupies their lives: construction worker, landscape architect, policeman, car salesman, store manager, librarian, doctor, teacher, or pastor. In my text Jesus, speaking of His Father, placed Him in a vocation and described Him in terms of His trade and work. He said, "My Father is a husbandman."

A husbandman is engaged in agriculture. He cultivates the soil, encourages the land to produce, fosters growth, and improves and refines his crops by labor, care, and study.

Describing God as a husbandman should be no surprise to the student of the Bible when you consider that both Old Testament and New Testament writing is saturated with farming words such as plowing, sowing, weeding, pruning, watering, grafting, "dunging," gleaning, harvesting, winnowing, reaping. Some of the farm implements are plows, sickles, pruning hooks, wagons, forks, axes. We read of oxen, yokes, and early and latter rains.

A husbandman's life has permanence, purpose, and patience. During the winter months he repairs equipment and farm structures and fences while planning what crops he wants and in which fields he will plant them. In early spring he buys seed or gets out the seed he has saved from the last crops, cultivates and fertilizes the soil, and then plants the seed. During the busy summer months he does not even think of leaving his tender plants to fend for themselves while he takes off on a six-week cruise or a camping trip to Colorado. No, he conscientiously guards his crops, controlling weeds and pests while waiting patiently for the "precious fruit of the earth" (James 5:7). Year after year, he stays focused on improving the soil and crop yield per acre, expecting his diligence to be rewarded. After the crops are in the barn or sold, he enjoys a great feeling of satisfaction. Now he can rest for a while until planting season comes again.

The antithesis of the husbandman is the nomad or vagabond. A nomad is a drifter without a permanent home. He wanders aimlessly, seeking only a better campsite or better grass for his cattle. When the grass is eaten down to the roots and the watering hole dries up, he simply takes down his tent, loads his personal belongings on a pack animal, and seeks another patch of grass on which his cattle or sheep can graze. He gives no consideration to restoring the land his animals have impoverished. He neither cultivates crops nor carries seeds for tomorrow. His future is always somewhere else. His life has no basis, no center. He is lonely and does not realize that his lifestyle is self-serving.

Cain started out as a husbandman. He tilled the soil, plowed, sowed, and reaped the harvest. He loved all aspects of agriculture and had built a home, a barn for his oxen, and fashioned a plow and other implements. His life had purpose and permanence.

But when God smiled on his brother Abel's animal sacrifice and frowned on his own offering of produce, instead of asking God how to regain His favor, Cain chose bitterness for his next crop. Soon it pushed down strong roots in his heart, and he fertilized them with resentment until the roots burrowed deep and produced a poisonous hate. Hatred motivated Cain to murder Abel.

Cain thought the problem was solved when he buried the body. He did not realize until too late that his extreme action had solved nothing. Instead, it threw him from the cauldron into the fire. Nothing would ever again be the same. God took away his occupation as a husbandman and sentenced him to the life of a nomad. This drastically altered his life-style, his residence, and his family ties. It relent-lessly pushed him into places he would rather not go and into circumstances he could barely tolerate.

"From now on," God said, "you will be a lonely wanderer. Wherever you go you will leave nothing of permanence behind. Your life and everything you own will have no basis, no center, no roots. You will find no rest and no peace." Cain said to God, "You have driven me out and hidden your face from me. I have no choice but to be a fugitive and a vagabond." Too late, Cain discovered that the only permanence in his life now was severance from God's favor.

A comforting truth for the branches that abide in the vine is that a husbandman does not expect his plants to produce fruit on their own. He carefully tends, nourishes, waters, and guards them. Neither does the divine Husbandman leave His plants to produce fruit on their own. His crop is *you*. You are "God's husbandry," "the planting of the LORD." (See I Corinthians 3:9; Isaiah 61:3.) If you abide in Him and He abides in you, you will bear much fruit (John 15:5).

To abide in the Husbandman means to dwell, to stay, to settle in, to sink your roots deep. The Husbandman knows you cannot produce fruit without His help (John 15:5). Without Him you cannot accomplish anything of permanent spiritual value. He wants the fruit, so He does not leave you to fend for yourself.

Where there is good fruit, you know there are good roots—and seeds for propagation. Jesus said, "A new commandment I give unto you, That ye love one another; as I have loved you, that ye also love one another. By this shall all men know that ye are my disciples, if ye have love one to another" (John 13:34, 35). The love of John 13:35 is pictured as fruit in 15:8. Displaying and sharing the love of God is an effective method of evangelizing the lost: "They [the lost] shall know" because you, as my disciples, are producing much fruit, the choicest of which is love. "That Christ may dwell in your hearts by faith; that ye, being rooted and grounded in love, may be able to comprehend with all saints what is the breadth, and length, and depth, and height; and to know the love of Christ" (Ephesians 3:17-19).

Jesus taught a parable of the sower. When the disciples asked what it meant, Jesus explained that the four kinds of soil represent hearers of the Word. "Wayside" hearers receive the Word but do not understand it. Their potential roots cannot penetrate the hard-packed soil, leaving the plants without anything to anchor them in God. The wicked one comes along and easily plucks them up, pulling the hearer away from the vine. "Stony place" hearers receive the Word with joy and their roots begin to grow downward. But to find enough soil for adequate nourishment, the roots have to circumvent stones, rocks, and boulders. While the roots strive to anchor and feed the plants, trouble comes and their weak resistance does not keep them from being pulled away from the vine. Some undiscerning hearers accept the Word into full hearts; unfortunately, they are full of aggressive briars and brambles. Soon thorns of worry and deceitfulness of wealth choke out the good seed and the hearer detaches from the vine.

Branches that disconnect from the vine dry up, turning brown and brittle. They do not settle in any particular field or bear one iota of good fruit. The Husbandman orders His helpers to gather the dead branches and throw them on the burn pile.

"Good ground" hearers stay attached to the vine. They hear the Word, understand it, establish a strong root system, and stay connected to the vine under the Husbandman's care. They produce much fruit. "Rooted and built up in him, and stablished in the faith, as ye have been taught, abounding therein with thanksgiving" (Colossians 2:7).

Look around you; become aware of the field in which you are planted. Is it dry, hard, and cracked; loaded with rocks and stones; full of briar patches that leach all the nutrients out of the soil? Or is it arable and fertile, well-watered and well-cultivated, weed-free and flourishing with healthy, fruitful plants? Good ground and much fruit glorify the Husbandman and make Him rejoice.

Chapter 5

The Cost of Coming Back

*A*nd he [Jacob] lighted upon a certain place, and
tarried there all night, because the sun was set;
and he took of the stones of that place, and put them
for his pillows, and lay down in that place to sleep.
And he dreamed, and behold a ladder set up on the
earth, and the top of it reached to heaven: and behold
the angels of God ascending and descending on it.
And behold, the LORD stood above it, and said, I am
the LORD God of Abraham thy father, and the God
of Isaac: the land whereon thou liest, to thee will I
give it, and to thy seed; and thy seed shall be as the
dust of the earth, and thou shalt spread abroad to
the west, and to the east, and to the north, and to
the south: and in thee and in thy seed shall all the
families of the earth be blessed. And, behold, I am
with thee, and will keep thee in all places whither
thou goest, and will bring thee again into this land;*

*for I will not leave thee, until I have done that which
I have spoken to thee of.*

*And Jacob awaked out of his sleep, and he said,
Surely the LORD is in this place; and I knew it not.
And he was afraid, and said, How dreadful is this
place! This is none other but the house of God, and
this is the gate of heaven. And Jacob rose up early
in the morning, and took the stone that he had put
for his pillows, and set it up for a pillar, and poured
oil upon the top of it. And he called the name of that
place Beth-el . . . And Jacob vowed a vow, saying,
If God will be with me, and will keep me in this way
that I go, and will give me bread to eat, and raiment
to put on, so that I come again to my father's house
in peace; then shall the LORD be my God: and this
stone, which I have set for a pillar, shall be God's
house. . . .*

*Then Jacob went on his journey, and came
into the land of the people of the east (Genesis
28:11–29:1).*

For Jacob, Bethel was a place of profound experiences. The first experience occurred when he was
forced to flee for his life after cheating his brother
and deceiving his father. He was on his brother's
hit list; he knew it was too much to hope that if he
stayed at home he would survive a confrontation
with a rugged man of the field like Esau.

Several days into his journey as the sun was
setting, he came upon a likely spot to spend the
night. In his haste to leave home, his mother had

failed to pack a bedroll so he used a smooth rock for a pillow and covered himself with his cloak. Exhaustion soon caused him to fall into a deep sleep, and he dreamed of a ladder that reached from earth to Heaven. Angels ascended and descended, drawing Jacob's gaze to the top of the ladder. There he saw a divine personage who said, "I am the LORD God of Abraham thy father, and the God of Isaac. I will be with you wherever you go and will keep you and bring you back to this place again. I will give this land to you and your descendents, and they will spread out from here in all directions and be a blessing to all the families of the earth."

All his life Jacob had heard of Yahweh, the God of his fathers, but since Yahweh was invisible—unlike the idols and images of other peoples—Jacob had always wondered if He was real. Now, like Isaac and Abraham before him, he had seen Yahweh and knew He was indeed real and was interested in what happened to him.

When Jacob awoke with the sun, the dream was still with him. He looked around the barren campsite, expecting to see something supernatural. Gooseflesh crept up his spine and raised the hairs on his neck. "I never dreamed God would be in a place like this . . . but He is. This is an awesome place, a wonderful and holy place, different from anywhere else. I will never forget what happened here." He called the place Bethel, the house of God.

The dream had refreshed him and changed his perspective. Hope that had died resurrected inside; maybe his life wasn't over. Maybe Yahweh would protect him from Esau. The God at the top of the ladder knew where he was and had promised to journey with him and provide for him. Maybe this great God would somehow restore the birthright and blessing he had obsessed over but now had lost.

Jacob lifted the rock his head had rested on, dug a hole, and set the rock on end to erect a pillar. He vowed, "If Yahweh will be with me, provide for me, and bring me back to this place in peace, He will be my God forever." Notice that even after his profound spiritual experience, the conniver couldn't help but stipulate what had to happen before he committed himself to anything.

As Jacob ate a cold breakfast, he kept thinking of the dream. If only he could stay here in Bethel . . . but there were too many unanswered questions and too many problems chasing him. He thought, "I sure do appreciate this place and what it has done for me. But to stay here right now would be too risky. I wouldn't survive if Esau found me here. I'll have to leave . . . but someday I'll come back."

Distance and time. That's what he needed. He had to get beyond Esau's reach. In his mother's childhood home, five hundred miles away from his family's home in Beersheba, he could prove himself. He needed a job and needed to find a wife so he could beget those descendents Yahweh had promised him.

He needed time. Maybe time would reduce to ashes the fire of his brother's wrath. Maybe the family would forget his trickery and forgive him. He didn't know what the time frame would be, but he promised himself to come back here—to Bethel. Padanaram was a good enough place to hide and work and start a family, but it would not be his permanent home. Someday he would come back to Bethel and fulfill the role of a patriarch like his grandfather and his father.

Like Jacob, those who leave Bethel, the house of God, do not intend to stay away forever. They are not sure how long they'll be gone, but they fully intend to come back. As Bethel disappears over the horizon, the longing to return is strong but time and distance weaken it. And, like Jacob, they ultimately find out that the cost of staying at Bethel, no matter what adversity that entails, is nothing compared to the cost of leaving and coming back.

Once Jacob found the house of his uncle Laban, he stayed for twenty years and worked for him, married two of his daughters, and begot children. His ingenuity and hard work amassed flocks, herds, cattle, camels, man servants, women servants, wealth, and fortune.

One day he overheard his brothers-in-law complaining to their father: "Look at what Jacob has done. He's cheated us out of our inheritance and left us with practically nothing! We've got to get everything back, but how?" After this, Jacob could tell that Laban's attitude toward him changed from commending his industry in building up the flocks, to complaining that the deal they made had played out unfairly for Laban's family.

Jacob couldn't believe they were calling him a cheat when Laban was the father of all cheaters! Not only had his father-in-law tricked him into marrying the unwanted sister before giving him the love of his life, that rascally skinflint had changed his wages ten times. Jacob made up his mind; it was time to go back to Bethel. God reinforced his decision when He said, "Go back to the land of your fathers and I will be with you."

He and his wives packed up everything and everyone and left. When Laban heard that his son-in-law had given him the slip, he pursued in a rage. How dare that scalawag make off with what rightfully belonged to Laban's family, lock, stock, and barrel? Only God's intervention prevented Laban and his sons from destroying Jacob and taking everything he had earned. Instead, they said their piece, made a pact, and went back to Padan-aram. Jacob headed toward Canaan.

The closer he got to Bethel, the stronger it pulled him there. But he also dreaded it because his brother's threat loomed larger with every step. Then a messenger told him Esau was coming to meet him with four hundred men! Did it mean that he still intended to kill him? What would happen when their paths converged?

Out of desperation, Jacob hatched a plan; maybe a generous gift would soften his brother's heart. He arranged for his servants to cull hundreds of his goats, camels, cattle, and donkeys and take them, one flock or herd at a time, to meet Esau. He also divided up his wives and children and instructed them to follow behind the animals, ford the brook, and approach Esau one group at a time.

As these plans were carried out, Jacob stayed alone on the other side of the brook and that night he wrestled with an angel, who, when Jacob would not loosen his hold on him, changed Jacob's name to Israel, a prince of God, because he "had power with God and with men" (Genesis 32:28). Jacob called the place "Penuel," the face of God.

The next day Jacob's fears proved to be unfounded. The gift had indeed softened his brother's heart, and they reconciled their differences. God had fulfilled His promise to be with Jacob and bring him again to his own land in peace. But Jacob was to find out that the peace came with a price tag.

Right then would have been a perfect time to continue on to Bethel, which lay to the southwest. Instead, Jacob took a straight westward course, possibly to follow a pass through the mountains that flanked the western banks of the Jordan River, and came to Shechem. He was impressed by the lush pasturage, and the Hivites who lived there seemed friendly. Jacob thought, "You know, this really isn't a good time to go back to Bethel.

Shechem seems like a great place to settle down, get a life, and raise my family. Here I can enjoy the success I worked so hard for in Padan-aram and build up my wealth even further." He bought some land, dug a well, and spread out his family among the heathen Canaanites.

Technically, he was obeying what God had commanded; Shechem was in Canaan, the land God had given his forefathers. Bethel was maybe twenty miles away—close enough. So he built an altar and called it El-elohe-Israel, the mighty God of Israel. He could be a patriarch here in Shechem.

Had Jacob forgotten his longing to return to the place where he first met Yahweh? As he did to Jacob, Satan sidetracks as many as he can from their journey back to Bethel. He attracts them with what looks like a prosperous place. He deceives them into thinking they will get along with the inhabitants. After they assimilate into the business and cultural milieu, it is almost impossible to find a good time to go back to Bethel. And those who get sidetracked find that their detour will cost them.

"But, Jacob," you might protest, "You've just come from Penuel where you met God face-to-face, and your relationship with Him moved into a deeper dimension. You've already come the better part of five hundred miles and are almost to Bethel, so why did you stop short of your original intention to go back? Yes, you've got the family and the home and the altar, but they're in the wrong place. I'm afraid nothing good can come out of this bad decision."

Sure enough, it wasn't long before the men in Shechem noticed Jacob's comely daughter Dinah. The chieftain's son seduced her. The next day he told his father he had fallen in love with Dinah and wanted her for his wife. For Jacob's family, this marriage would mean permanent, close ties with people who didn't know or worship Jacob's God.

Jacob's sons met with the Hivites to discuss a deal for intermarrying with them on one nonnegotiable condition: the heathens had to submit to circumcision, a sign of the Jewish covenant with God. The Hivites thought this a small price to pay to trade with the Israelites, share in their prosperity, and intermarry with them. They did not know that Dinah's brothers, Simeon and Levi, hated them because they felt their sister had been treated like a prostitute. Their parley with the Hivites had a hidden motive. Before the men could recover from their circumcision, Simeon and Levi entered the city and slaughtered the men, looted their businesses, ransacked their homes, and stole all of their animals.

Jacob nearly came unhinged when he heard what his vigilante sons had done. "I would have stopped you if you had told me your plans!" He tongue-lashed them, "Don't you and the rest of my sons have any fear of God? Are you crazy enough to think we can stay here after what you've done? We've become a stench in the nostrils of everyone in the area. They will all band together and destroy us! Now we've got to pull up stakes again."

Sadly, the patriarch Jacob, who had been raised to acknowledge and fear the one true God and who had made a vow to him at Bethel, had failed to communicate any godliness to his family. His wives and children had no concept of Jacob's God. They knew only the ways of the world and the heathens around them.

The treachery of Simeon and Levi in Shechem is one proof of this. Another example involves his beloved Rachel. As they were leaving Padan-aram, she swiped her father's household gods and hid them in her camel's saddle. Some ancient Mesopotamian documents seem to indicate that these household deities, about the size of a child's doll, served as title deeds, the possessor of which received the major share of the family inheritance. Some think Rachel took the gods to ensure a prosperous journey. In any case, she wanted gods she could see, not some invisible Someone Jacob occasionally mentioned.

Somewhere along the way back to Bethel, Jacob was shocked to see Rachel setting up her gods and recognized them as the ones that had sat in a sacred niche in Laban's home. No wonder Laban had been so mad! Now, as they prepared to flee from Shechem, Jacob insisted, "Get rid of your foreign gods, Rachel, and every one of you purify yourselves and change your clothes." This washing of their persons and changing of clothes signified repentance and starting a new relationship with Yahweh based on honesty and inward character. If Jacob had taught his family to believe and trust in Yahweh, his wife would have left the gods in Laban's house. If he truly intended to go back to Bethel as soon as he reached Canaan, he would have performed these symbolic acts of repentance after his experience in Penuel.

Jacob did not care if Rachel found it hard to give up her gods in order to make a clean start in Bethel. Likewise, we have to want a right relationship with God and His house so much that it overrides our "gods": compulsions, desires, addictions, and appetites. Those former things don't belong in Bethel, and it would do no good to go there without getting rid of them, no matter how hard it is to say good-bye. Jacob buried the household gods under an oak tree in Shechem, and they began the journey toward Bethel.

Yet the price of coming back continued to escalate. The older brothers vented their jealousy on Joseph, Jacob's favorite son, by selling him into slavery. They dipped his special coat into the blood of a goat and brought it to their father, letting him think Joseph was dead. Some of the brothers were involved in other misdeeds that brought further shame on Jacob's family and his God.

But Jacob was finally ready to fulfill his patriarchal role as priest of his family. He built an altar in Bethel and called it El-beth-el, the God of the house of God. Now his awe was not only for the place, but he fell in love with the God of the place.

What draws a person back to Bethel? Is it the beautiful building, the pastor, the saints, the singing and worship, the Sunday school teacher, or the spiritual treasures and provision? No, those things are not enough of a draw to keep you there, and the price of coming back is wasted when you leave again. Returning to Bethel and staying there happens only when you fall in love with the God of the house of God. Only a passionate love for the God of the place will keep you in that place.

You might ask, "If the cost of coming back to Bethel is so great, why should I come back at all?"

Coming back is worth the cost because there are some things in Bethel you cannot find anywhere else: peace, security, truth, unconditional love, fellowship, support, help in time of need, and your own ministry niche. However, only your love for the God of the house of God will keep you there and help you to become like Him. He is the source of all the good things in Bethel. His favor rests on those who stay there. Most important, He is the only One who can give you eternal life. Of course, life in Bethel is not without its problems, challenges, and adversities, because Bethel is not in Heaven. However, God is our counselor, problem-solver, helper, and champion.

Build an altar in Bethel. Establish an intimate relationship with the God of the house of God. Doing so will make you a godly influence on others.

Until Jacob went back to Bethel and built the altar El-beth-el, his religious leanings had no impact on his wives or his children. His vow made during his first experience in this place reveals that his reverent attention was more about the place than about the God. His desire to come back and stay was conditional; only if Yahweh would go with him, protect him, feed him, clothe him, and—the big one—bring him back to Bethel in peace, then Yahweh would be his God.

This time at Bethel, building the altar and consecrating himself and his family to God brought about some profound changes as the years passed. Jacob's dedicated life began to impact his sons, especially Joseph and Benjamin, the youngest two. Joseph and Benjamin were Rachel's children and seemed to be the only ones, up until now, on whom Jacob had the greater influence. After Joseph was gone and as the years passed, even the older brothers made some positive changes in their lives, evidenced by how they acted when they finally encountered Joseph in Egypt.

Yes, staying in the house of God will cost you some heartaches and challenges, but the cost of leaving is always much greater, even when you make up your mind to come back. How much more profitable it is for you and those around you to stay in Bethel, even when problems and adversities arise. How much better it is that on the first heavenly encounter there, you fall in love not only with the house of God but with the God of the house! The profit far outweighs any cost.

Chapter 6

In Adam

*A*nd the L*ORD* God formed man of the dust of
the ground, and breathed into his nostrils
*the breath of life; and man became a living soul
(Genesis 2:7).*

*For since by man came death, by man came
also the resurrection of the dead. For as in Adam
all die, even so in Christ shall all be made alive (I
Corinthians 15:21-22).*

The idea of the soul has fascinated men of
every religious conviction and yet eludes any sort
of firm definition. The soul of man has been the
subject of endless debate, and volumes have been
written concerning the origins and meaning of the
soul. Instead of solving the quandary, all the debate
churns up the water, which seems to get muddier
with each added opinion.

I don't have the definitive answer to the question of the soul, but neither does any living human.

The subject is too illusive, like a person looking at his reflection in a rippling creek, or too shrouded in mystery, like trying to find your way home in a pea soup fog. However, we can deduce a few things on the subject based on biblical references. Some of the writers of Scripture cleared away the fog for just a moment to shed a little light on the human soul so we can catch a glimpse of what it all means.

We'll start with Moses' account of the Creation. God created countless varieties of all forms of life: fruit trees and herbs, some for food for man, some to color his world; all manner of fish species, even some mammals that live in the oceans; thousands of kinds of birds, including some flightless varieties; and all sorts of land animals, including reptiles and insects.

The First Adam

But when it came to creating humankind, God made only one man and called him Adam.

God created the universe by the power of His spoken word. But when it came to creating humankind, He got down in the dirt and formed the man. In the man he put organs like the brain, heart, lungs, and liver. He put in place a circulatory system, respiratory system, and a digestive system. He gave form to the creature by fashioning an ingenious skeleton with movable joints. He put muscles on the frame so the creature could move his limbs, bend his torso, lift, even smile and blink. But nothing would work without a system to coordinate everything, so He added a nervous system.

With all of that creative genius invested in him, the creature still lay inert in the dust. There was no self, no personality, no desire, no delight, no passion, no will, no personhood, no hunger, and no blood. Adam still had no soul.

When God leaned down and breathed into Adam the breath of life, only then did man become a "living soul." Just as he had a spirit but was not a spirit, he did not so much "have" a soul as he was now a living soul.

- Life's breath leaves the body at death, but the soul is different from the body in that it is not dissolved in death.
- The soul is as real and as vital as the flesh.
- The soul gives a person a sense of self apart from the body, and a personality.
- It is the seat of feelings, desires, affections, appetites, emotions, passions, and will.
- In the soul is the essence of the mind, will, and character.

Adam's soul issued out of the breath of God's own life. If God gave it, He could take it away. He declared sole ownership of the inner being of man: "Behold, all souls are mine; as the soul of the father, so also the soul of the son is mine: the soul that sinneth, it shall die" (Ezekiel 18:4).

In this sense, God was the Father of Adam's soul. And when Adam had his first son, God breathed into him the breath of life, then into each son and their children . . . and into every human that has ever been born alive. He has never relinquished His sovereign ownership of the souls of humankind.

Scripture speaks of a hungry soul, a weary soul, a thirsty soul, a grieving soul, and a living soul. These are kindred expressions of the inner self, the soulish part of man, as opposed to the flesh of the body. The body will perish, but the soul is what needs saving. James wrote, "He who converts a sinner from the error of his way shall save a soul from death, and shall hide a multitude of sins" (5:20). "Receive with meekness the engrafted word, which is able to save your souls" (1:21).

Peter wrote, "Receiving the end of your faith, even the salvation of your souls" (I Peter 1:9).

When Adam entered consciousness, it was like coming out of a void of nothingness. His life sprang forth out of death. The beauty of his life emerged out of barrenness. He became a living soul.

"Living" denotes sustenance and the promise of a long line of family members and descendents. Humans "live" in community, a body of persons with a common history.

I submit this premise: In a sense, Adam was more than just his unique soul, his own blood, his singular personality and character. Within himself he carried more than his own desires, his own passions, his own will, and his own personhood.

Just as an acorn contains within itself all the potential of the entire oak tree—its trunk, limbs, bark, leaves, roots, and sap—Adam within his body, soul, and spirit was the world and everyone who would ever be born. Adam is the root from which we all sprang.

It was as if God said, "I will take this one life, one passion, one desire, one will, one emotion, one breath, one blood type, and make all souls, all nations, and all cultures, until time shall be no more." (See Acts 17:26.) No one is exempt from the one blood; as the community of Adam, we are all interrelated.

If my premise is true, the entire world, from the moment Adam became a living soul until the last baby is born on earth, is "in Adam."

Implications for All Humankind

The man Adam must have been a splendid being.

Science tells us that every human has genetic material that was handed down to him from past generations through his genes. Genes are the basic unit of heredity. They are the basis for biological inheritance. They carry the information, potential, and blueprint with which we were built. Genes carry human traits, talents, gifts, and abilities. Each person's distinguishing qualities and attributes emerge out of his or her genetic makeup.

If my logic holds up, then "in Adam" was the entire host of genetics of everyone who has ever been or ever will be born. Within him was the potential for every talent, gift, art, craft, skill, endowment, expertise, intelligence, ability, and mental power.

This magnificent human specimen was made in God's image and likeness and was designed and purposed to glorify God through obedience to His word and will. But Adam deliberately disobeyed and fell short of what he knew would please and glorify God. This unworthy act polluted and defiled every talent and trait of every human that would come after him.

In this sense, all humanity was driven from the presence of God when Adam had to leave the Garden.

Adam lost his position in God's favor, he forfeited his place in the Garden, and he lost all fellowship and communion with his Creator. Adam's sin set the course for every soul that would populate human history. For example, in himself Adam carried the potential of the following notable representatives of humankind who were gifted in various ways:

1. *Plato*: In Adam was Plato, teacher of Aristotle and disciple of Socrates. This Greek philosopher's idealistic exposition, *The Republic*,

still has great impact on philosophy and political theory, and it still guides the progress of higher thought. When Adam was driven from God's presence, Plato went with him. His ability to analyze and explain problems, values, and disciplines of logic could not restore his status with God. His brilliant philosophy could not save him.

2. *Michelangelo*: This gifted Italian sculptor, painter, and architect was one of the greatest influences on the world of art. He spent four years painting twelve thousand square feet of the ceiling in the Sistine Chapel. He also painted *The Lord's Supper* and sculpted Moses and David. But the splendor of all these righteous accomplishments could not earn him the right to entertain the presence of God.

3. *William Shakespeare*: He was one of the greatest poets and dramatists of history. Many of his plays are still in print and on the stage: "Romeo and Juliet," "A Midsummer Night's Dream," "Hamlet," and so on. Swept along with Adam's misfortune, Shakespeare's giftedness in drama could not save him.

4. *Ludwig van Beethoven*: Beethoven was a German composer who spent his musical career in Vienna. He is one of the most respected and influential composers of all time, his name being synonymous with classical music. Among his works are thirty-two

piano sonnets, ten violin sonatas, and nine symphonies. But because he was in Adam, even the wonder and thrill of his musical masterpieces could not keep him from being separated from God.

5. *Albert Einstein*: He was a theoretical physicist best known for his theory of relativity, specifically mass-energy equivalence. He developed the quantum theory and the modern concept of the photon as the fundamental unit of electromagnetic radiation. In 1921 he won the Nobel Peace Prize in physics. But no display of genius or education could bring his lost soul back to God.

6. *Sports stars*: When God drove Adam out of the Garden, he took with him the entire NBA, the NFL, the Olympic athletes, and the boxing and baseball greats. All of their agility, hand-eye coordination, strength, speed, or power will not help them fight their way back to God.

7. *Money magnates*: Warren Buffett, Bill Gates, Jim Walton, and Michael Bloomberg have a combined wealth of $163 billion, yet in Adam they were all driven from God. Their extreme riches will not buy their way beyond the flaming swords or bribe the cherubim guarding the gate to Eden.

By one man sin entered the world. One man's failure and disobedience put us all under Adam's curse (Genesis 3:17-19). We all became sinners, and death was passed upon all humankind. We don't have to repeat Adam's sin or replicate his disobedience; we're guilty by virtue of being in Adam.

"But there's no justice in any of that," we might object. "It seems so unfair. I feel like I've been victimized." We can lament our condition, but it won't change it. Even if we could stop sinning, we'd be just as lost. Because we're members of the Adamic community, we took part in his disobedience and separation from God.

The Last Adam

There is only one hope for a soul lost in Adam, and that is Jesus Christ, because "in Adam all die, even so in Christ shall all be made alive. . . . The first man Adam was made a living soul; the last Adam was made a quickening spirit" (I Corinthians 15: 22, 45). The "last Adam" is Jesus, and His life will have a much greater impact on the destiny of humankind than that of the "first Adam," or any other human after him. For the "quickening spirit" of the last Adam means He is a life-giver. He is able to save the soul lost in the first Adam.

How can this be? How can we get out from under the stigma of the first Adam?

Nicodemus, a ruler of the Jews and curious about this "second Adam," approached Him tentatively: "Rabbi, we know that thou art a teacher come from God . . ." But Jesus went straight to what Nicodemus needed to hear:

> Except a man be born again, he cannot see the kingdom of God. Nicodemus saith unto him, How can a man be born when he is old? Can he enter the second time into his mother's womb, and be born? Jesus answered, Verily, verily, I say unto thee, Except a man be born of water and of the Spirit, he cannot enter into the kingdom of God. That which is born of the flesh is flesh; and that which is born of the Spirit is spirit. Marvel not that I said unto thee, Ye must be born again (John 3:3-7).

The only way to escape from the penalties of the first Adam's sin is to be born again of water and of the Spirit; this new birth takes us out of the first Adam's community and places us in that of the second Adam, Jesus Christ. Through His obedience to God's will and His self-sacrifice, he reversed the condemnation and death for those who were in the first Adam and gave abundant, eternal life to those who are born into His own community. There is no condemnation for those who are in Christ (Romans 8:1).

This new birth involves water and Spirit—water baptism and infilling of the Holy Spirit. What must we do to participate in this new birth?

Then Peter said unto them, Repent, and be baptized every one of you in the name of Jesus Christ for the remission of sins, and ye shall receive the gift of the Holy Ghost. For the promise is unto you, and to your children, and to all that are afar off, even as many as the Lord our God shall call (Acts 2:38, 39).

There is neither Jew nor Greek, there is neither bond nor free, there is neither male nor female: for ye are all one in Christ Jesus. And if ye be Christ's, then are ye Abraham's seed, and heirs according to the promise (Galatians 3:28, 29).

We were all one in Adam, shared in his disobedience, and inherited his curse. But through the miracle of new birth—spiritual birth from above—we are made one in Christ and can share in His inheritance of eternal life. We are all one in Christ Jesus and made to be partakers of His resurrection.

The first Adam is the father of the flesh, but God is the Father of the soul. All bodies have been born of the flesh, but only those who participate in the new birth have been born of the Spirit. Those who remain in Adam have only a second death to look forward to (Revelation 21:8). But the wonderful news is that through the second Adam, a person's soul can be saved and he can be restored to a right standing and communion with Christ. In essence, Revelation 20:6 says that the second death has no power over those who are in the second Adam, Jesus Christ.

Chapter 7

Surviving the Taking Away

While he was yet speaking, there came also another, and said, The Chaldeans made out three bands, and fell upon the camels, and have carried them away, yea, and slain the servants with the edge of the sword; and I only am escaped alone to tell thee. While he was yet speaking, there came also another, and said, Thy sons and thy daughters were eating and drinking wine in their eldest brother's house: and, behold, there came a great wind from the wilderness, and smote the four corners of the house, and it fell upon the young men, and they are dead; and I only am escaped alone to tell thee. Then Job arose, and rent his mantle, and shaved his head, and fell down upon the ground, and worshipped. And said, Naked came I out of my mother's womb, and naked shall I return thither: the LORD gave, and the LORD hath taken away; blessed

be the name of the LORD. *In all this Job sinned not, nor charged God foolishly (Job 1:18-22).*

Every child of God probably has a slightly different perspective of God. When we attempt to characterize Him, we might consider His qualities, perhaps those that distinguish Him from other gods. Or we might try to list His attributes or traits that most express His nature.

From my own perspective, I see our great Lord and Savior primarily as both the Gift and the supreme Giver. The gift of His only begotten Son is the greatest sacrificial gift of love man has ever known. Because God is love, He gives until it hurts.

If anyone asks, God will give him an answer. If anyone seeks, God makes sure he finds. If anyone knocks, God will open the door to him (Matthew 7:7-8). Out of His benevolence He can satisfy everyone.

How could anyone help but fall in love with such a giving God? His sacrificial, loving generosity is so attractive that it draws sinners to Him. By it He has won the allegiance of hundreds of thousands. I suppose that many a church has been built through emphasizing the loving, giving nature of God.

I hope the above premise makes it crystal clear that I am not casting a shadow on the Giver when I bring to you a take-away message. I know that it is neither popular nor palatable to speak of God as one who takes away. A take-away message does not draw crowds or attract the masses. This perspective of God does not seem to kindle revival fires or inspire Holy Ghost crusades. A take-away message is hard even for saints to swallow. We tend to shun the idea and lock it away in a vault because it leads to unexplainable hopelessness.

Job knew intimately the giving side of God's nature. As Job's great wealth increased so did his influence; he commanded the respect of everyone throughout the countryside. Besides material wealth, he had seven sons and three daughters.

But one day—all in this one day—he discovered that God had a counter trait. As a bewildered Job heard message after message that shattered his whole world, the rusty dial turned and the door of a dusty vault creaked open. All along, this truth had been hidden in a corner of the vault, swathed in the cobwebs of Job's neglect. Now he saw the stark truth: God not only gives but He also takes away.

Throughout his ordeal, Job repeatedly asked God why: "Why then did you bring me out of the womb? I wish I had died before any eye saw me. If only I had never come into being, or had been carried straight from the womb to the grave!" (Job 10:18-19, NIV). After a lifetime of receiving, he could not comprehend why it had all been taken away.

I cannot explain in detail why God takes away, but I have discovered that at times the taking away, although devastating, is absolutely necessary for the purpose of God to be fulfilled.

"He said, Sacrifice and offering and burnt offerings and offering for sin thou wouldest not, neither hadst pleasure therein; which are offered by the law; then said he, Lo, I come to do thy will, O God. He taketh away the first, that he may establish the second" (Hebrews 10:8-9).

If He takes away the first, there is a second on the way! When God "establishes the second," He sets your life in balance, places you in a favorable position, puts you on a firm footing, makes your faith firm, causes you to grow and multiply, and brings better things into existence. Therefore, the taking away is not designed to hurt, wound, or break you, but rather to add something better to your world.

For example, God took away Lot to establish Abraham. He took away Ishmael to establish Isaac. He took away Esau to establish Jacob. He took away Joseph to establish the nation of Israel. He took away Moses to establish Joshua.

It is a biblical principle illustrated time and again: God must take away the first in order to establish the second. In effect, He says, "I know you're hurting right now, but if I don't take this away, there won't be room in your life for Me to add something better. Be assured that I will redeem and restore you because you need these 'second' gifts in order to grow and multiply."

For thirty-five chapters Job asked God why. He endured the misunderstanding and unfair accusations of his friends and the mockery of those who had once respected him until he wished he had never been born. He mourned the loss of his children and suffered the agony of debilitating fevers and grievous sores. Worst of all, he could not understand why God would not answer him or reveal His whereabouts. It seemed as if God had utterly forsaken him. When his wife could no longer bear his suffering, she urged Job to give up and end his own life. Job knew that was unnecessary; he was going to die anyway, and it would not be long until he did. He said to his so-called friends, "Where then is my hope? Who can see any hope for me? Will it go down to the gates of death? Will we descend together into the dust?" (Job 17:15-16, NIV).

Yet through the horror that Job's life had become he clung to a few certainties and remembered that he did have a shred of hope after all. Underneath all the agony and disillusionment, Job knew that God still lived and would "redeem" him, that is, vindicate his case, even if it didn't happen until after Job died. He knew that even if his body wasted away with disease, he would someday see God with his own eyes. He said, "How my heart yearns within me!" (Job 19:27, NIV). Even though he was in despair because He couldn't find God, still, he reminded himself, "He knows the way that I take; when he has tested me, I will come forth as gold" (Job 23:10, NIV).

Toward the end of Job's ordeal, God did not explicitly explain to him that He had taken away in order to give more. But after his circumstances began to improve, Job realized that his "why" questions had been answered. God had taken everything away in order to give him something better.

What did Job receive that was better? His health was fully restored, his flocks and herds doubled, his wealth multiplied, and he regained even greater respect in his community. He learned to pray for his friends, forgive their abuse, and reestablish relationships with them. Most important, he learned more about God: God was always in control, even when it appeared that He wasn't. Job now saw God's love in both the giving and the taking away. He had become a better, wiser man.

Elisha was confused and bewildered when he learned God was about to take away his master, Elijah. (See II Kings 2:5-6.) What would he do without his teacher and confidant? How would he know where to go and what to do without Elijah's guidance? Would he be in danger of falling without his safety net?

After his first fledgling attempts at ministry, Elisha came to understand that he didn't really need the safety net of Elijah; God would catch him if he fell. When he established his own relationship with God instead of relying on Elijah's, he would know where to go and what to do. He could confide in God, and God would be his teacher and master. He discovered that he had not lost Elijah's example; he could still hear the echoes of his master's voice with the right advice at the right time. During the span of his ministry, Elisha realized that God had truly given him what he had asked for: a double portion of Elijah's spirit. He now understood that God had taken away the first to establish the second.

We read in the Book of Ruth about a famine in Judah. Desperate to provide for his family, Elimelech took his wife, Naomi, and their two sons out of Bethlehem, "the house of bread," and went to Moab in search of better job opportunities and food. But it did not work out as Elimelech and Naomi had planned. Naomi learned that the road to Moab had actually been a death march and that Moab was a land of funerals. God took away all of Noami's "firsts," her husband, and then her two sons. She was left with two Moabite daughters-in-law, Ruth and Orpah. Naomi thought that what she had now was much, much worse than what she had at first.

She wished she had died along with her husband and sons. Why go on? There was nothing left for her in this strange, pagan land but grief, want, and rejection. She felt no relief at all when she thought of her two foreign daughters-in-law. Her hope had been taken away, her future collapsed, and her destiny destroyed. Surely the Lord's hand was against her.

But then she saw a feeble glimmer of hope. She heard that Yahweh had restored bread in Bethlehem. She packed up and started on the journey back to her own people. But how could she rid herself of the unwanted daughters-in-law? They said they would go to Judah with her but did she really want them to? "Go back, each of you, to your mother's home," she urged. But they insisted they would accompany her. "Return home, my daughters," she repeated. "Why would you come with me? I'm too old to marry again and have more sons for you to marry. I've lost everything—what has happened is bitterer for me than for you. You're still young; you'd be happier in Moab with husbands of your own people."

Orpah finally agreed, kissed Naomi, and headed back home. Naomi urged Ruth, "Look, your sister-in-law is going back to her people and her gods. Go back with her."

Ruth said, "Don't urge me to leave you. I want to go where you go. Your people will be my people and your God my God. When I die I want to be buried beside you." Naomi began to realize God hadn't deserted her after all. He was extending His kindness to Naomi through the loving, steadfast heart of this Moabite girl.

When the women of Bethlehem saw Naomi coming down the road, they did not recognize her; sorrow had etched deep lines in her face and put a stoop in her back. And who was that woman with her? She was surely not an Israelite, for her clothes betrayed her. When they finally recognized Naomi they were shocked at the change in her. What had happened? And where were her husband and sons?

"Welcome home, Naomi!" they called. Naomi, aware that her name meant "pleasant," did not feel

that way at all. Bitterness exuded from her counte-
nance and tainted her words and actions. "Don't call
me Naomi. Call me Mara, because the Almighty has
made my life very bitter. I went away full but the
LORD has brought me back empty."

Naomi and Ruth did their best to clean up the
deserted family house. When it was livable, Naomi
turned her attention to Elimelech's land lying fallow
in the hot sun. How would they live? Ruth offered,
"I'll go out and glean in the fields of nearby farms."
Naomi was again surprised that the girl, instead
of depending on her, wanted Naomi to trust her to
bring in food to sustain them. It was another indica-
tion that God had not taken everything away without
giving something back.

Ruth happened upon the abundant fields of Boaz,
a kinsman of Elimelech. Naomi was delighted when
she heard that Boaz had shown interest in Ruth and
had given her special treatment. The happy girl
always came back with her sack loaded with grain.
As Boaz's interest in Ruth grew, Naomi began to
think of Boaz in the role of her kinsman redeemer.
Would he be interested in redeeming Elimelech's
inheritance? But that would mean he had to take
the young Moabite widow for a wife. Would he be
willing to taint his family's lineage with foreign
blood?

Indeed, he would. Boaz married Ruth and when
their first son, Obed, was born, Naomi thought of
him as her own. Noami's heart overflowed with

love and gratitude. Her bitterness disappeared. Boaz was a generous protector and provider; what a comfort to know the Lord had not left her without a kinsman redeemer! Naomi's friends told her that Obed would renew her life and sustain her in her old age. And as for Ruth, she had proved her love for Naomi. Her friends said of Ruth, "She is better to you than seven sons!"

Rather than ruining the family tree, Obed became the branch that bore Jesse, the father of David. Boaz and Ruth's lineage was honored because their descendents included Jesus, the Messiah. God had taken away the first that He might establish the second.

The first is temporal and limited in time. The second is spiritual and eternal. The transition between the first and the second hurts so much; we think it will last forever. We grieve and mourn for everything we once had.

Hebrews says the first law, the law of Moses, was temporary. Jesus' coming and claims confused and hurt the Jews. They felt at sea without the traditions and trappings of their ancient law. Many of them were afraid to switch allegiance to the second law, the law of Christ. But the first had to be taken away in order to establish the second. Instead of on tables of stone, the second law would be written on men's hearts. It would be established forever.

When He establishes the second, God restores joy. The second is fresh, permanent, durable, stable, and constant. Those who survive the taking away learn so many things about God they could not have learned any other way. They now know in an intimate way that the love and faith and hope He gives are everlasting. God is kind and will sustain and provide. He satisfies longings and gives His people what they thought they would never have again. He guides and teaches and invites confidences and relationship. His people delight in greater spiritual riches and a fresh revelation of God.

Only those who survive the taking away discover that the second is so much better than the first!

Chapter 8

The Journey from Waste to Want

A nd he said, a certain man had two sons: and *the younger of them said to his father, Father, give me the portion of goods that falleth to me. And he divided unto them his living. And not many days after the younger son gathered all together, and took his journey into a far country, and there wasted his substance with riotous living. And when he had spent all, there arose a mighty famine in that land; and he began to be in want (Luke 15:11-14).*

Since the time Christ walked the earth none of His stories has been so loved and preached as "The Prodigal Son." With this story Jesus portrayed the family relationship between a father and his two sons. Although the main emphasis of the story is the father and his amazing compassion and forgiveness, I want to focus on the younger son, whom I'll call Jared, and tell you how much fun he had when he could finally do whatever he wanted and go wherever he wanted. How then did he end up in a place much worse than he had ever been and be forced to do repulsive things he would never have dreamed he would do?

Growing up, Jared had been a hyperactive scamp, always getting into mischief, always saying the wrong thing without meaning to. Being the youngest, he wasn't required to shoulder the heavy burden of responsibility his older brother carried. From an early age, Jared was taught that his brother would someday inherit two-thirds of their father's assets, and that meant his brother shared with Father either the blessing of increasing wealth or the blame when it dwindled. The older brother worked long and hard beside his father to build up the farm that he, in effect, already owned. But instead of working from dawn till dusk, Jared did only as much as he was forced to do and the rest of the time managed to disappear from the fields or the barn so he could hang out with his best "buds." In spite of everything, he viewed himself as Daddy's favorite.

By the time Jared approached the last of his teenage years, Dad's rules had chafed him raw, and if he heard one more criticism from his greedy brother, he would knock him out. He just had to get away from all the demands and the ridicule and the fault-finding he thought he didn't deserve. If only he were far away where no one could tell him what to do. But by what chance could that pipe dream ever become a reality? He spent every idle moment trying to think of a way to make it happen.

Then he hit on an outrageous plan that just might work. He could ask Father to give him his share of the inheritance right away instead of waiting until — you know what. Even though it was only one-third, it would surely be more than enough to have a very good time with no one looking over his shoulder. Jared ignored the fact that no upstanding, respectful Jewish son would ever think of asking such a thing. According to the Jewish law of inheritance, such an act could only be initiated by a father and never by a son. But he assumed his dad would let him make his own decision — after all, he was always harping at him to grow up. And he didn't care what anyone else thought.

He asked to speak to his father privately. When they were alone Jared said, "Father, I'm sorry, but I want out of here. I'm old enough to be on my own, and I can make it if you'll do one thing for me. . . ." It came out in a rush: "I'm asking you to give me my share of the inheritance — I mean — right now."

This part of Jesus' story must have shocked the first-century Jews. How could a son be so cruel as to ask for his share of his father's inheritance before the man was dead? How would the father react to such an outrageous request?

Jared's demand stabbed his father's heart. He thought, "Hasn't the boy learned anything I've taught him? Why does he always have to kick over the traces and run away? Is he so unfeeling that he can't wait for me to die?"

Jared took his father's silence as a sign of assent. "Good, Dad. I knew you'd see it my way. When can I put my land and goods up for sale?" Jared would slash the asking price so everything would go quickly. The sooner he got the cash and got out of here the better.

Of course, someone snapped up the bargain. It came extra cheap because it would be held in trust until the father's death. As soon as Jared closed his fist on the money, he was out of there.

He didn't even care what road he took; he simply loved the delicious taste of freedom. He threw his money around, becoming a high roller, admired (or so he thought) by all his new friends. He was so glad Dad wasn't there to tug at the reins and ruin everything; he could blow his money any way he wanted and invite everyone to enjoy it with him. All his friends loved his spontaneity, his capacity for pleasure, and his willingness to take their advice on the best way to have a good time. All he had to do was party—and foot the bill.

Jared indulged himself in acting out all his fantasies. "This is great!" he exulted. "I've never had this much fun. Wait till I tell my brother I've done things he's never even thought of. Now I'm a man, and he's still a kid doing everything Dad tells him to do. What a brown-noser."

What Jared's immaturity didn't let him see was that underneath the chaos and wild spending was a hard, painful knot of unhappiness and loneliness. He refused to recognize the ache of homesickness. And he would never have believed it if someone told him his friends were abusing him.

One day he woke up with a splitting hangover. He got out his wallet and suddenly realized it was flat; he was broke. How had his money disappeared so fast? No matter—he was sure his friends would be as generous to him as he had been to them. But he was devastated when he showed them his empty wallet and they just laughed and one-by-one turned him down. They called him a loser and a chump. His happy-go-lucky façade shattered. Now what would he do? Surely he had never intended to come to *this* place.

Finally hunger drove him to admit he'd have to get a job. But doing what? At home he'd never learned how to do anything except get out of doing anything. But surely some of his dad's money-making talent had rubbed off on him. However, every business owner he asked shook his head; they didn't need or want someone with no training or experience. As his hunger and weariness increased, he became desperate.

Then he had an idea. Farming. He hated farming, but he'd seen how Dad did it. He was sure he knew how to do it too. He'd talk some farmer around here into hiring him as a field worker or something.

Anyone could plow a field or fork hay. At this point he'd do anything to get a decent meal.

But every farmer said he didn't need any more hired help. Until Jared came to a ramshackle farm the likes of which he would have despised when he lived at Dad's house. As he made his way up the rutted lane, he disdained the seedy looking house and fields overrun with weeds. No one answered the door, so he went around to the barn.

When Jared asked about a job, the farmer looked him up and down and started to shake his head, but he suddenly changed his mind. "Come to think of it, I've got the right job for you. Cross that fence there," he pointed to a fence on the far side of the barnyard, "and the field hand will tell you what to do." He turned and went back to work.

Jared trudged across the barnyard. The closer he got to the fence the more his nose wrinkled involuntarily. The air reeked of *pig*. He'd never be able to stomach the smell. Father would never keep such disgusting animals. He would just have to try to ignore the smell if he wanted this job. He couldn't believe it when his stomach gave a loud rumble as he climbed over the fence. How could he possibly feel hungry while standing in this wretched field, hearing the offensive grunting and snorting, and breathing the fetid air?

When he told the field hand why he was there, the wizened man looked at him incredulously. "You want to work *here*?"

"The farmer said to go to this field and you'd show me what to do."

Comprehension dawned on the man's face and he grinned; this fool was going to take over the part of his job he hated most. "Oh. He meant you're now the official pig-slopper. Here, I'll show you where to get the mash and the scraps." As the field hand tutored him about the pig-feeding process, he said, "Since we're fattenin' these porkers up for sale, feed them twice a day," and walked away leaving Jared on his own.

Jared worked gingerly, trying not to touch anything or step in anything, but it was impossible. He knew it wouldn't be long before he smelled like a pig and was as dirty as one. After he finished the ordeal, he wondered when supper was. As time went on, no one called him. He saw the field hand drop his bucket and head for the house, so he followed him. But the farmer stopped him at the door. "What d'*you* want?"

"I thought it was time to eat," said Jared.

"I offered you a job, not free food. Where or what you eat doesn't concern me." He shut the door in Jared's face.

What now? He'd have to have something soon or he wouldn't have enough strength to work. He went back to the shed where the farmer's wife dumped the scraps. How could he even think of eating any of it? But he had to have something and that's all there was. He scrounged through the revolting scraps and found a few edible morsels. Just the thought of eating garbage made him gag, but he finally managed to swallow a few bites.

The next day Jared realized that if something didn't change soon, he could starve to death. That thought shocked him. He looked around and saw where he was living—with pigs! This was not right. He'd never meant to end up in a place like this doing what he didn't want to do. Nothing had turned out the way he planned. He was so mixed up.

That night he spread a rough sack on some hay and lay down. In the twilight zone between wakefulness and sleep, a picture of home swam into focus. A shocking surge of homesickness and longing welled up and tears stung his eyes. He couldn't believe that what once had seemed so stern and distasteful now seemed comforting and appealing. He wished his father would come and find him. "Fat chance," he thought bitterly. "Now I know he always liked Older Brother best."

The more Jared thought about it, the more he realized he had to go home. Swallowing his great lump of pride and shame would almost be harder than swallowing the garbage. But he thought, "I'd far rather work in Dad's fields than in this disgusting place. Maybe if I really beg he'll hire me, even though I deserve to be nothing more than a servant. . . . I can't wait to taste the good food at home!" He got up and walked away from the shed without looking back.

On the way home he grew faint and exhausted; he wished he hadn't gone quite so far when he left home. At last he approached his father's farm. He stopped short when he saw Father coming down the lane. He didn't know what to expect: Would Dad bellow, "Turn around and march right back where you came from!" Would he yell, "I *knew* it would come to this. Now you expect me to take you in again after what you've done!" The repentant son caught his breath in surprise, then joy, when Dad broke into a run with his arms spread wide, tears streaming down his face. "Oh, my son! Why did you wait so long to come home?"

Wrapped in his dad's arms, Jared discovered he now knew some things he'd refused to learn while he was still in his father's house:

1. He learned that his dad had been right not to chase after him and drag him home. Father knew his younger son would never be happy at home until he chose to live there.
2. He learned how awful it felt to disappoint Dad and tarnish the family name. But Dad didn't say, "You're a mess and a disgrace. I hope you know it was no one's fault but yours." Even though Jared knew he was unworthy of it, when he begged his dad's forgiveness, his father immediately gave it. Then he knew how clean and comforting it felt inside to be in a right relationship with his father.

3. He now accepted the fact that there were consequences for his actions. His inheritance was gone—scattered to the four winds—never to be retrieved. But it was still good to be home. And father would supply all his needs and pay him a good wage.

4. He had been in the far country longer than he really wanted to stay, but he knew he could never be gone long enough for his family to forget him.

5. As he passed one mile marker after another, he couldn't believe how far he'd gone to get away from Dad's disapproval and Brother's disagreeable ways. But now he knew that he hadn't gone so far that he couldn't find the way back home. He'd even been glad to see his brother!

6. He now saw Dad's boundaries and constraints as safety and protection instead of irritating confinement. In the far country what he had thought of as freedom was actually bondage and degradation in disguise. Being wild and free wasn't all it had cracked up to be. The party scene had no more substance than tumbleweeds scurrying in the wind.

7. He learned the difference between the real love at home and the artificial love of his friends in the far country. He knew whom he could trust to stay with him through thick and

thin; being surrounded by his family's love meant everything to him now.

8. When it was time for the feast Jared's mouth watered as he looked at the meats, vegetables, fruits, and homemade bread. He saw how foolish he'd been to suffer want in the far country. There was always something good to eat in Dad's house!

Chapter 9

The Keeper of His Presence

*T*he men of Kiriath-jearim came, and fetched up the ark of the LORD, and brought it into the house of Abinadab in the hill, and sanctified Eleazar his son to keep the ark of the LORD. And it came to pass, while the ark abode in Kiriath-jearim, that the time was long; for it was twenty years: and all the house of Israel lamented after the LORD (I Samuel 7:1-2).

At the top of Mount Sinai God gave Moses the tables of stone graved by His own finger. Since Adam's fall God had longed once again to commune with His people, and the time had come to establish a covenant with them. Both sides had to bind themselves to the terms.

God fully intended to fulfill His own responsibilities: "If ye will obey my voice indeed, and keep my covenant, then ye shall be a peculiar treasure unto me above all people" (Exodus 19:5). He promised, "I [will] send an Angel before thee, to keep thee in the way, and to bring thee into the place which I have prepared" (Exodus 23:20). All of the people answered, "All that the LORD hath spoken we will do" (Exodus 19:8).

To symbolize His presence dwelling in their midst, God designed the Ark of the Covenant. It was a rectangular wooden chest not quite four feet in length and twenty-seven inches in depth and width, and overlaid with gold within and without. Around the top a golden crown outlined the Mercy Seat, which signified the dwelling place of the glory of God. Flanking the Mercy Seat were two glittering cherubim that guarded it and whose outstretched wingtips touched each other. The ark was an emblem, a token, a visible image of the invisible God. It assured the Israelites of God's guidance, protection, healing, and provision.

Inside the ark were the Ten Commandments (the divine Word of God), a pot of manna (divine provision of God), and Aaron's budding rod (the divine power of God).

Once a year, on the Day of Atonement, a lamb was slain for the sins of the people and its blood sprinkled on the Mercy Seat. Israel had "broken" the Law. When Yahweh looked down on the broken commandments, He was blinded by the blood that paid the price for Israel's transgressions. Yahweh's mercy triumphed over judgment, and He pardoned Israel's sins.

Therefore, without question, the ark was the most precious thing Israel possessed; without it nothing else mattered. The ark was life to His people.

But something happened in the 450 years between Mount Sinai and the end of the time of Israel's judges. The Israelites forgot their resolve to hold up their end of the covenant. For all practical purposes, the ark had lost its meaning and significance. Most Israelites thought of it as we would think of a spare tire—in case of emergency, they brought it out as a last-ditch option, thinking it would serve as a good luck charm. They were unfaithful to Yahweh and provoked His anger and jealousy with their high places and graven images. (See Psalm 78:57-58.)

We see this illustrated in I Samuel 4:3-11. Toward the end of Eli's ministry as judge and high priest, Israel went out to fight against the Philistines, thinking it was a sure win. But the Philistines routed them and Israel suffered four thousand casualties. God's people could not understand why He had not given them triumph as He had in the past. Someone came up with the idea to take the ark with them out to the battlefield; maybe their luck would take a turn for the better. When Hophni and Phinehas brought the ark into the Israelite camp the Hebrew warriors shouted wildly, thinking they would now prevail.

The Philistines were confused by the war whoops that sounded like a victory celebration. Why weren't the Israelites mourning their fallen warriors? But the Philistines were not confused about one thing:

Israel's God had a great reputation among the heathen. The Philistines had been awestruck when they heard all the stories about His deliverance and protection of His people. Then their recon men discovered their enemies had brought the ark into the camp, and their fear escalated to panic.

"We're in trouble! We don't stand a chance against their god's mighty power. We'll end up serving the Hebrews unless we can get our hands on that ark!"

The Philistines were almost surprised when they won the ensuing battle, killing thirty thousand more men. They captured and slew Hophni and Phinehas and brought the ark triumphantly back to their own camp.

They celebrated their victory, not realizing the only reason they won was that Yahweh had withheld His hand. Sadly, Yahweh would rather go home with the enemy than go home with Israel. He "forsook the tabernacle of Shiloh . . . and delivered his strength into captivity, and his glory into the enemy's hand" (Psalm 78:60-61). He had warned His people when He first established the covenant that their failure to abide by the terms would release Him from His side of the covenant. Now His patience had worn dangerously thin.

When the aged Eli heard the news of his sons' deaths and that the ark had been captured, he fell and broke his neck. Phinehas's wife was laboring to deliver a child, and the dire news of her husband's death caused her own death, but not before she named her son Ichabod, "the glory has departed."

Still celebrating, the Philistines paraded the ark back to Ashdod and set it their temple next to Dagon. But during the seven months it stayed there, the men of Ashdod were smitten with a strange, gruesome malady. Realizing that the disease had broken out at the same time they captured the ark, they decided they had had enough. They cursed the wretched box and loaded it upon a cart hitched with two cows that complained as they pulled it back to Beth-schemesh. (See I Samuel 6.)

The Israelites were overjoyed to see the ark approaching. In their excitement, they pried open the lid to see what was inside. They paid for that major mistake with the lives of fifty thousand men. Struck with fear, they decided they did not want the ark any more than the Philistines did, and called for men of Kiriath-jearim to take it away. To the Philistines the ark had become a cursed disease. To Israel it had become a widow maker.

- Thirty-four thousand footmen died when the ark was taken.
- Eli and his sons died.
- Phinehas's wife died.
- When the ark came back, fifty thousand more Israelites died.

Israel had attended 84,004 funerals all because of this old box. They were glad to foist it on Abinadab in Kiriath-jearim. Abinadab had three sons, Eleazar, Uzzah, and Ahio (I Samuel 7:1; II Samuel 6:3). Surely between them they could "keep the ark."

The young men understood what it meant to keep the ark. The responsibilities involved appropriate conduct, faithfulness, establishing a relationship with it, and conforming to what it stood for. It entailed support, preservation, maintenance, defense, and confining oneself to the holiness associated with the ark.

The boys may have said, "But we're neither priests nor Levites. We're not trained for this. Besides, no one else wants it, so why should we have to keep it? We've got plans, friends, dates, school, dreams, and ambitions. If we keep the ark, we'd miss all of that. Who wants to put their life on hold for God knows how long? This is simply too much to ask."

But then, as Eleazar looked at the ark, awe and conviction struck Him. Suddenly he knew what he had to do. "I'll do it, Dad. I'll reprioritize my life, alter my commitments, and reset my goals. I'll lay down my dreams and forfeit my ambitions to be the sanctified keeper of the ark of God's presence and glory."

While his brothers enjoyed their youth, Eleazar's commitment cut the core out of his life. Anyone he associated with had to be comfortable in the presence of God. It affected his behavior, choice of a mate, friends, or any position that would not be compatible with the presence of God. He kept his vow to protect, shelter, honor, and guard the ark.

No king, priest, tribe, people, or nation wanted the ark. For twenty years Eleazar was the only custodian of the divine Word, the divine provision, the divine power, and the divine presence.

Twenty years elapsed. David, who was now the king, set his heart on bringing the ark to Jerusalem. He erected a special tent to lodge it until a permanent structure could be built, and took a great entourage of people to Abinidab's house so they could celebrate on the triumphant journey back to Jerusalem.

Ignorant of the proper way to transport the ark, they, like the Philistines, set it on a new cart for the journey. It is not surprising that Uzzah and Ahio jockeyed into position to escort the ark, not considering that it was their brother's due. When no one had wanted the ark, they shunned it; now that everyone wanted it, they grabbed the limelight. It was show time!

Along the road to Jerusalem a wheel of the cart must have gone over a rock or sunk into a rut. Cumbersome and heavy, the ark shifted and Uzzah reached out to steady it. As soon as his fingers touched the ark, Uzzah fell to the ground dead. The entire procession halted and a deadly quiet descended. What had gone wrong? Why was Yahweh so angry when all they wanted was to give the ark a place of honor in the City of David? Could Uzzah be lying dead on the ground because he had presumed to touch the sacred ark even though he had not consecrated himself to keep it? Confused, David aborted his plans and lodged the ark at Obed-edom's house where it stayed for three months.

Somewhere during that time, David discovered the proper way to transport the Ark was on the shoulders of the priests, and they brought it to Jerusalem with great rejoicing. The ark rested in its temporary tent home for about forty years.

After Solomon became king, he purposed to build the Lord a magnificent Temple. At its completion, the priests brought the ark, set it in the Holy of Holies, and the glory of the Lord filled the house. The priests would now be the keepers of the ark.

The point is that throughout Old Testament history, someone kept the ark for you. Someone forfeited his will for your benefit. Someone gave up his earthly dream for your heavenly hope. Someone laid down his life that you might enjoy abundant life. And someone gave up his present to secure your future.

In Solomon's dedicatory prayer, he asked the Lord, "That thine eyes may be open toward this house night and day, even toward the place of which thou hast said, My name shall be there: . . . And hearken thou to the supplication of thy servant, and of thy people Israel, when they shall pray toward this place" (I Kings 8:29-30). The presence of God finally had a permanent dwelling in the midst of

His people. Now they could call on him in times of trouble, sickness, failure, or backsliding, and know that He would hear.

"The Lord is thy keeper" (Psalm 121:5). God can be trusted to keep His side of His covenant with you. He will be faithful, act consonantly in relation to you, support, preserve, maintain, watch over, defend, and tend to you. He is eager to establish a relationship with you. And He is committed to your security and well-being.

Jesus prayed, "Holy Father, keep through thine own name those whom thou hast given me. . . . I pray . . . that thou shouldest keep them from the evil. . . . Sanctify them through thy truth" (John 17:11, 15, 17). The Greek word for "keep" means to keep watch, guard from loss or injury, keep an eye on. Like the newly delivered children of Israel and like Eleazar, we must be sanctified in order to keep the covenant.

On your part, He asks that you "keep" that which He has committed to you (II Timothy 1:12). Here "keep" means "prevent from escaping." Unlike Israel, you can choose to faithfully keep His commands. Then you will have the privilege of being the keeper of His presence. Then you can claim the promise that He will keep you. "And the Lord is faithful, who shall stablish you, and keep you from evil. And we have confidence in the Lord touching you, that ye both do and will do the things which we command you" (II Thessalonians 3:3, 4).

Chapter 10

The Sea Never Rests

*B*ut *the wicked are like the troubled sea, when it cannot rest, whose waters cast up mire and dirt. There is no peace, saith my God, to the wicked (Isaiah 57:20-21).*

There is something compelling and yet disturbing about the sea. We flock to its sandy shores by the droves. When someone says "vacation" many think of some coastal resort or seaside condo.

There is something tranquil about the ocean's vastness. The sound of waves lapping at the shore seems to relax us and lull us to sleep. Some of the remaining so-called paradises on earth are islands surrounded by crystal-clear, emerald waters. We conjure a picture of palm trees, gentle trade winds, white sands, cloudless skies, tropical sun, and coconut-shell halves filled with frosty lemonade garnished with a little umbrella. Hey, anybody want to go with me?

Inlanders have more experience with lakes and ponds than they do with the sea. There are times when a lake is as smooth as glass—calm, placid, peaceful—without a ripple or a wave. But the sea is not so; it never rests. It knows no peace. Even when it is relatively calm, it is constantly in motion.

The sea can be temperamental: moody, unpredictable, angry, impulsive. It can change at a whim of the wind. The only sure thing is . . . it never rests.

In Indiana where I live, the sea is not an everyday part of life. It comes to my attention only when it produces some horrendous disaster. I'll never forget the hurricane season of 2005 when Katrina first began to brew over the Bahamas. She cut a swath across Florida, churned up the Gulf of Mexico, and devastated the coastal areas of Louisiana, Texas, and Mississippi. She was labeled as one of the deadliest hurricanes in U.S. history, in which 1,836 people died and another 705 went missing. The destruction cost more than $100 billion. Some residents still have not been able to rebuild their homes.

Besides a hurricane, another oceanic disaster is a tsunami. In 2004 an undersea earthquake in the Indian Ocean measuring a 9.2 magnitude caused a megathrust that killed 230,000 in eleven countries. It created waves up to one hundred feet high and sounded like a train hurtling 300–620 miles per hour. Its epicenter hit Sumatra, Indonesia, and pushed far inland, washing away entire cities and burying people under mud and debris. When the sea vents its fury it does so with deadly force.

In spite of the disasters associated with the sea, most of the time it stays out of the headlines and the front-page news. Except for the getaway vacation luring us winter-weary northerners to its sandy shores, we take little notice of the sea.

But even when there is no tsunami, no hurricane, or no storm surge, the central characteristic continues: the sea never rests. It is always working, never idle; always agitating and never making peace. I suspect that when the sea is not making the news highlights is when it is doing its most subtle work.

In Isaiah 57:20-21, the sea refers to the wicked. They cannot rest or find peace; their waters constantly stir up mire and dirt. Jude uses a similar metaphor for the wicked: they are "raging waves of the sea, foaming out their own shame" (Jude 13). Wickedness rises to the surface everywhere, in both the spirit world and the temporal world. Jude cited angels that left their first estate, demons, evil spirits, and principalities. In the temporal world he cited the perverted sinners of Sodom and Gomorrah, fornicators, and filthy dreamers that defiled the flesh.

No, the wicked can find no place to rest. They never cease from their labors but they relentlessly pursue evil. They may not make the evening news, but under the surface they are still moving with the currents, causing violent upheavals and oceanic swells, destroying everything in their path.

One example of the effects of the relentless sea is Cape Hatteras on the Outer Banks of North Carolina. The Outer Banks comprise a two-hundred-mile string of narrow barrier islands. The Atlantic currents of this area are ideal for ships—except for around the Diamond Shoals extending ten nautical miles into the sea. Here the warm Gulf Stream current collides with the colder Labrador Current, creating powerful storms and sea swells. So many ships have run aground, including the Civil War ironclad *USS Monitor*, that the area has earned the title "Graveyard of the Atlantic."

In 1870, the Cape Hatteras Lighthouse was built 1,500 feet from the pounding waves. For 129 years, day in and day out, each relentless wave carried away a few grains of sand until one day the public finally became alarmed—the sea had devoured more than 1,300 feet of the shore and was threatening the lighthouse from only 150 feet away! The devastation was not caused by a tsunami, but by the relentless agitation of the sea.

The wickedness of the world is the sea, ever beating against us, the church. We too can be worn down, our joy, our dedication, and our holiness eroded away by the relentless lapping of the waves. Lulled by the constant roar and rhythm of the waves, we become oblivious to the danger of the encroaching sea. Sometimes we don't become aware of the threat until it's almost too late.

There is hardly anything in North American culture that pushes a person closer to God. Capitalism, entertainment, the Internet, television, amusement parks, shopping malls, vacations, talk radio, social networking sites, and everything else that attracts the eye or the ear or the interest is often diametrically opposed to spiritual life. The items on this list are not necessarily "evil," but, like the waves that pound the beach, if we are constantly preoccupied with them their relentless beating will wear away our sensibilities as well as our spirituality.

John said, "Love not the world, neither the things that are in the world. If any man love the world, the love of the Father is not in him. For all that is in the world, the lust of the flesh, and the lust of the eyes, and the pride of life, is not of the Father, but is of the world" (I John 2:15-16). Inspired wisdom says one cannot love God and love the world—or the things that are in the world—at the same time. But when there are no emergency weather bulletins, warning signs, and headlines, we never notice the ever-narrowing strip of land that separates us from the world.

If we do not love the world or the things that are in the world, why do we debit-spend to get bigger and better things? And after we get them, why do we still envy those who have more? Why do we fry our eyeballs, wasting endless hours surfing the Net or playing video games or vegging in a hypnotic state in front of the television? Why do we blow money on amusements and cruises? Why do we bombard our senses with rock or country or rap or whatever else the world calls music?

What would saints of old think about the institution we now call Christianity? What would the great revivalists think? What would the apostles think? How far from the relentless sea did these Christian pioneers build the church? And how far is it now?

When the people realized the sea was threatening the existence of the centuries-old Cape Hatteras Lighthouse, they moved it, at great cost and effort, a half-mile inland. But the problem now was it was so far away from the dangerous Diamond Shoals that although its beacon shone as brightly as ever, it was too far away to warn ships of the peril. Ships could maybe see the light, but it wasn't close enough to show them where the danger lay. It was as if the sea resented the beacon's saving light and slowly but surely rendered it ineffective. Now there was no warning from the guardian of the death trap of the Atlantic. Instead of performing a vital service to seafarers, the relic of a lighthouse now became a tourist attraction and a museum.

The apostle Paul said, "What do righteousness and wickedness have in common? Or what fellowship can light have with darkness? . . . Therefore come out from them and be separate" (II Corinthians 6:14, 17, NIV). But how literally should we take this? Do we live in an isolated compound or on a mountain somewhere? Jesus said to His disciples, "I have chosen you out of the world" (John 15:19). But He also said, "My prayer is not that you take them out of the world but that you protect them from the evil one. They are not of the world, even as I am not of it . . . As you sent me into the world, I have sent them into the world" (John 17:15-16, 18, NIV).

Therefore we are not to withdraw so far from the world that those in trouble cannot see our shining light, but while we are doing that we are to remain separate from the world's system, attitudes, propensities, and evil. If we move the church too far inland, its light will be too feeble to help a person escape the jutting rocks and churning currents. Its remoteness from its purpose will turn it into a monument to what it used to be. No, the church must stay where it is close enough to the world for its light to show the way to safety, but it must erect a sturdy seawall to protect itself from the world's subtle erosion.

The church's seawall protects from the darkness of wickedness while at the same time allowing our light to penetrate that darkness. Without the safety of this wall, our spirituality begins to erode away until our own survival is questionable. Then we won't be of any help to those who are venturing too close to the treacherous shoals.

The beacon light of the church is threatened not only by erosion, but also by storms. In 2003, Hurricane Isabel, the costliest and deadliest that year, bombarded the east coast from South Carolina to Maine. The whirling dervish with winds up to 165 miles per hour formed a tropical wave that hit Cape Hatteras and washed out a 2,000-foot-wide swath of land, forming Isabel Inlet. Forty-five percent of the Outer Banks population had to be evacuated, and damage in North Carolina was estimated at $450 million. But the lighthouse still stood.

Jesus told a parable of the wise and foolish builders. Foolish built his house on the sand and the storm washed everything away. Wise built his house on the rock, and the same rains, floods, and winds had little effect. The house remained standing because it was embedded in the Rock.

The seawall we erect around ourselves protects us from erosion, but our foundation in the Rock adds His strength to ours and forms a protective barrier against the violent storms that attack the church. With the church maintaining the seawall and God providing stability and further protection, our light will continue to shine.

Jesus said He was the light of the world. He came not to judge, but to save. Instead of withdrawing from the sinful, the diseased, and the broken, He walked among the ones who needed Him the most. He didn't draw away in disgust but touched lepers, ate with publicans and sinners, talked with the wayward Samaritan woman, delivered the Gadarene madman, and marveled at the faith of the Gentile woman who begged for help for her daughter. He "rubbed shoulders" with uncleanness, wickedness, and debauchery, but none of the dirt clung to Him. He was in the world but not of it.

Following His example, we hate the wickedness of the world system and take no part in it. But we move among its needy people. We don't climb to the superior height of the lighthouse and stay there looking down with judgment on the unfortunate, but with humble compassion we seek to warn, help, and save those who are blindly heading for the dangerous shoals. Like Jesus, we are not aloof but approachable. Not condemning but compassionate. Not isolated but involved. In this way our light will continue to shine.

Chapter 11

When the Doing Is Done

O our God, . . . we have no might against this great company that cometh against us; neither know we what to do: but our eyes are upon thee. And all Judah stood before the L<small>ORD</small>, with their little ones, their wives, and their children. Then upon Jahaziel, . . . a Levite of the sons of Asaph, came the spirit of the L<small>ORD</small> in the midst of the congregation; and he said, Hearken ye, all Judah, and ye inhabitants of Jerusalem, and thou king Jehoshaphat, Thus saith the L<small>ORD</small> unto you, Be not afraid nor dismayed by reason of this great multitude; for the battle is not yours, but God's. . . . Ye shall not need to fight in this battle: set yourselves, stand ye still, and see the salvation of the L<small>ORD</small> with you, O Judah and Jerusalem: fear not, nor be dismayed; to morrow go out against them: for the L<small>ORD</small> will be with you (II Chronicles 20:12-17).

Without question, we are a generation of doers. We believe that something can and must be done about every adverse aspect of life, whether it is health-care, global warming, illegal immigration, terrorist threats, drug abuse, or disease. The desperate cry is, "Somebody do something!" Some will answer the plea, "We are doing all we can."

Doing is not necessarily a bad thing, because most of what we know we learn by doing. We benefit from every good thing our predecessors have done. I appreciate the "doers" who work in laboratories, hospitals, or research centers, and teachers, inventors, scientists, or entrepreneurs whose "doing" benefits mankind.

I am also thankful for every church, pastor, Sunday school teacher and helper, and for all saints who want to do something for the Lord. "Doing" for His kingdom is the greatest ambition and goal of life. There is no higher calling.

"Do" is a verb that shows action, and most people are action driven. This tiny word is power-packed; it denotes making it happen, producing a desired result, dealing with it, defeating it, and so on. All of this doing is part and parcel of the human mind. If given enough time, money, and resources, we assume we can do something about any circumstance regardless of how complex it is.

"When the Doing Is Done" was born out of the distress of a father over his dying son Cory. Cory's cancer was the most aggressive case the doctors in several hospitals had even seen. His body was swollen with fluid and racked with pain. He couldn't sleep or eat and the smell of food made him sick. They couldn't drain off the excess fluid for the tangle of cancer cells had metastasized, affecting his digestive tract and internal organs.

Finally the doctors gave up trying to restore Cory's health. They told Spencer there was no further treatment for his son, no surgery, no medicine, no cure, no hope.

Spencer had struggled in mortal combat against unseen foes. He said to me, "I've prayed every prayer I know to pray. I've come against demonic strongholds. I've cursed the darkness and the disease and claimed God's promises of healing. I've fasted, repented, begged, pleaded, and even bargained with God. I've taken Cory to the best doctors. I don't know what else to do."

I tried to reassure him. "You've done a good job taking care of Cory—finding the best medical facilities and treatment and trying your best to make him comfortable. You've done everything possible, as much as lies within you." I paused. "But Spencer, there's nothing more you or anyone else can do. I'm afraid the doing is done."

I am convinced, through personal experience and helping others, that the single most trying time is when we have to face the fact that "the doing is done." We have tried every possible solution and consulted every person we think might be able to help, but nothing and no one can make it happen. The desired result is still elusive; the problem cannot be defeated. It seems our situation is beyond the scope of human doing.

That's when the "doing" is absolutely and positively "done."

The question that begs an answer is, What, if anything, can anyone do when the doing is done?

Second Chronicles 20 relates the story of a national crisis in Judah. The great armies of Moab, Ammon, and Edom had confederated and, like a destructive tidal wave, threatened to engulf Judah's military force. King Jehoshaphat and his army might have defeated any one of these individual armies, but they were helpless against the united horde of bloodthirsty men. It would be a massacre. There was nothing they could do and unreasoning panic took over.

Weak and paralyzed by fear, Jehoshaphat called for a nationwide day of fasting and prayer. People from every town in Judah flocked to Jerusalem and assembled before the Temple. Jehoshaphat took a position in front of the courtyard and led the prayer. He praised God for His power and recounted the time when God had driven out the Canaanites and given Israel the Promised Land. He prayed, "We have inhabited this land and built a sanctuary for Your name. Whenever we were overwhelmed by calamity, we cried out to You. But now the armies of Ammon, Moab, and Edom have allied and are marching against us."

He reminded God, "When we left Egypt, we obeyed Your command not to invade the territories of Ammon, Moab, and Edom. Now how are they repaying us? They are threatening to take away our inheritance! We do not know what to do, but we're trusting that You will tell us." A hushed silence descended on the people.

Out of the quietness they heard the voice of Jahaziel, the head of the twentieth course of priests. "Don't be intimidated by this vast army, for the battle is not yours, but God's." He told them where to find their foes, and his next declaration and instruction whisked away their panic. "You will not have to fight this battle. Take a firm position and see the deliverance God will give you. The Lord will be with you!"

Overcome with relief and awe, the people sank to their knees to worship and the Levites broke into loud songs of praise. Their stress and fear was suddenly transformed into joy now that their God was in control, not Ammon and Moab and Edom. They didn't know how He would do it, but they were sure they were now looking at a victory instead of a defeat.

The next morning they set out. They climbed the mountain, wending their way through the pass and toward the Jeruel Desert. Jehoshaphat had not powwowed with his generals about battle strategy.

He had not given the men weapons or prepped them for the battle. He knew that on their own they didn't have any more chance of surviving than a lamb against a lion. He had to relinquish the role of commander-in-chief and give the position to God. So Jehoshaphat sent the singers to the front of the marching column and they led the people in praising God for victory.

What they didn't know was that as they marched and sang, a vicious argument escalated in the enemy camp. I imagine that Edom, because of its haughty pride, had assumed they would make the decisions and lead the battle. In any case, fighting broke out between the two factions, and after Ammon and Moab had slaughtered Edom, they turned on each other and didn't quit until the last man was dead. All Judah had to do now was gather up the spoil. They were amazed at what God had done!

Moab. God despised that heathen nation. His disdainful metaphor for them was, "Moab is my washpot," not fit for much but washing people's dirty feet. During the time of the judges, Naomi, a woman from Judah, found herself grieving over the deaths of her husband and two sons. They had come to Moab because of the famine in Judah, thinking they would stay awhile, work to recoup their losses, and build a small nest egg. By then the famine in their homeland would be over and they could return to Bethlehem.

Those plans disintegrated when Naomi had to bury her men in Moab's alien soil. All she had left were two heathen daughters-in-law whom she did not consider as family. Now the only thing she could think to do was go back to Bethlehem where she belonged. She wished they had never left, famine or no.

One daughter-in-law decided to remain in Moab, but the other one, Ruth, somehow got it in her head that she would accompany her mother-in-law back to Judah. She didn't let Naomi's prickliness dissuade her from clinging to her. Something in happier times had attracted her to Naomi and her God, and she was determined to venture into an unfamiliar land.

After they got settled in Bethlehem Ruth wondered what she could do to support her aging mother-in-law. Then she remembered Naomi had told her Jewish law required that farmers not reap the edges of their fields so needy people could glean the grain. Ruth asked Naomi's permission to glean and set out to find a likely field. She happened on one of Boaz's fields and her beauty and diligence caught his eye. He knew Naomi, this woman's mother-in-law and Elimelech's widow; Elimelech had been his kinsman. From the day he found out who Ruth was, he looked past her ethnic origins and saw her loyalty to Naomi and her eagerness to do whatever she could.

From that point in the story, Ruth laid aside initiative and did everything she was told to do.

Boaz told her to glean exclusively in his fields and invited her to eat the noon meals with him. She did. After Ruth came home several days loaded with grain and talking of Boaz and how kind he was to her, Naomi picked up on his attraction. Even though he was somewhat older than Ruth, he would make a good husband and provider. She told Ruth to bathe in scented water, put on her best clothes, go to the threshing floor where Boaz slept to guard his harvest, and lift Boaz's cloak off his feet so he'd wake up and notice her. Naomi said, "Don't worry; when Boaz wakes up, he'll tell you what else you should do." The next course of action would be out of Ruth's hands as Boaz assumed responsibility for conducting the business of redeeming Elimelech's inheritance. Ruth had obeyed everything Naomi told her to do and it was up to Boaz to do the rest.

The people in all three of these examples, Spencer, Jehoshaphat, and Ruth, did everything they could do and it still wasn't enough. Like these people, our limitations hem us in. After we've done everything we can think of to do and everything others advise us to do, we feel frustrated and hopeless when the desired end is not reached. Finally we must confess, "The doing is done."

I've learned through both example and experience that the bottom line is this: we are responsible for obedience and action in doing what we can, but God is responsible for the results.

Cory finally reached the limit of his endurance; the doctors didn't know how else to help him, and his family could pray no more. Just before he died he lifted his hands to Heaven and said, "We win!" How could he declare victory when he knew he was dying? Because he realized that his God whom he loved and who loved him was in control, and He would take care of the family he was leaving behind. He trusted that whatever happened to him in the afterlife would be the right thing.

Jehoshaphat did all he could do—pray and obey. He won not by fighting, but by doing what God told him to do and praising Him for whatever the result would be.

Ruth did everything she could do, clinging to Naomi and her God, traveling to a strange land, and gleaning in the fields to support herself and her mother-in-law. She did what Naomi and Boaz told her to do. Then she transferred to Boaz's hands the responsibility for whatever the outcome would be.

When the outcome is not what you expected or wanted, you have not failed. Don't feel guilty about not doing more than you did—you did everything you could until you reached the limit. That's when you must relinquish the feeling of responsibility for the outcome and place it in God's capable hands. When He accomplishes the result He desires, it may leave you either hurting or rejoicing but you can trust that He did the right thing. No matter what the outcome is, though, your trust in Him blesses you with a peace and calmness you could never have achieved through your own doing.

Chapter 12

Hast Thou Found Honey?

Hast thou found honey? Eat so much as is sufficient for thee, lest thou be filled therewith, and vomit it (Proverbs 25:16).

Possibly every Christian falls into a funk at times. That's only human; no one can float on cloud nine twenty-four seven. But sometimes we start to enjoy visiting the State of Funk and take up residence. We're the only ones who can fully appreciate what it's like living there, so it's mulligrubs and misery. Then misery is more fun if shared, so into every sympathetic ear we pour a litany of our struggles and afflictions.

Sometimes we, who are on the inside of Christianity, develop the mindset that the Christian life is meant to be lived in depression, oppression, and repression. It's shriveled souls, wounded spirits, and weary bodies. Unfortunately, when the put-upon insiders tell the outsiders what it's like in there, the outsiders look in the window and say, "That's not for me. Too much of a pain." Any brightness that might try to penetrate their darkness is blocked.

Solomon, in Proverbs 25, wrote of some kingdom problems: dross in the silver, false witnesses, wicked unfaithful men, brawling women, boasters, enemies, and backbiters to name a few. This sounds like some people's assessment of the church. But tucked into the chapter is a question: "Have you found any honey?" On your journey through the kingdom did you bump into anything desirable, enjoyable, or sweet? Have you caught sight of anything delightful about living for the Lord? Did you stumble upon any shred of happiness or joy or pleasure?

It is true that pleasure can have both positive and negative aspects. Some love pleasure more than they love God. Some are choked with the cares and riches of this life. Some would rather enjoy the pleasures of sin for a season than wait until God's time to grant real pleasure.

The positive side of pleasure is that when God gives it, He pours it out in rivers: "How priceless is your unfailing love! Both high and low among men find refuge in the shadow of your wings. They feast on the abundance of your house; you give them drink from your river of delights" (Psalm 36:7, 8, NIV). His sweet pleasures last forevermore (Psalm 16:11).

Unlike some people's view of living for God, He does not deny us pleasure. Pleasure is not forbidden fruit. He does not say, "If you encounter any honey, any happiness, any joy, or any sweetness in My kingdom, be sure to stay away from it because it is sinful and unholy. I'll be ashamed of you if you eat it." No, He says, "If you find honey, eat enough of it to satisfy you" (Proverbs 25:16). "Go ahead and enjoy it. All I ask is that you not eat more than is good for you, because too much honey will make you sick."

What are you looking for in God's kingdom? Do you view it as a land of beauty and promise, or as a wasteland? As the Israelites wandered in the wilderness, they spent a lot of time and energy complaining about what they found. They knew that upon their departure from Egypt God had promised to give them a pleasant land flowing with milk and honey, but in all the desert's heat and barrenness and weariness they couldn't "see" the Promised Land or even the miracles God performed to deliver them from Egypt and to keep them alive. All they did was murmur about the water, gripe about the food, ignore the rules, and dance around the golden calf.

Moses told them, "God will give us the Promised Land for our inheritance. It is an abundant land, an agreeable land, a rich land. There's plenty of room to grow." He did not hide the fact that the Canaanites and all the other "ites" lived there, so to get the land they would have to wrest it from them. But none of that seemed to sink in; they were too focused on their discontent.

When they finally arrived on the threshold of the Promised Land, Moses sent in twelve men to spy out the land. Two of them came back extolling the land's productivity and its beauty. They urged, "Let's go in right away! Sure, there are imposing, fortified cities, and even some giants. But we are well able to overcome them!"

Ten spies threw a huge wet blanket over the zeal and optimism of the other two. "Don't listen to the hype. There are giants everywhere in that land—everyone we saw was taller and stronger than we are. Compared to them we look like grasshoppers. They'll squash us as soon as we set foot in the Promised Land!"

The contagion of cowardice and fear spread throughout the camp. They didn't believe they would ever conquer the land or taste the sweetness of victory. All they could see was the opposition and taste the bitter herbs of their fear of it. Exasperated and angry, God turned them around and marched them right back into the wilderness. They must have derived a twisted joy out of griping because they did a lot more of it for forty years. They never saw as much as one beehive.

Then there are those who do find some honey. Samson went down to Timnath intent on becoming betrothed to a young lady he had met there. He had just come to the beautiful vineyards of Timnath when a lion leaped out from nowhere and roared at him. In a split second, Samson realized he was defenseless; he had not thought to bring a weapon because he was courting the girl he wanted. Looking around, he didn't see anything with which to defend himself against the threat.

Suddenly the Spirit of the Lord came upon him and with a roar of his own he leaped at the lion, tore apart its jaws, and in a frenzy cracked its bones and bashed its head in until the lion lay in a mangled heap. Samson got up and continued on, excited about what awaited him at his destination. The subject of the lion no longer registered; all he could think about was enjoying the trip and seeing the girl.

The lion-killer did not gripe about his ordeal to the girl or her parents or even his own parents. He did not complain, "Why me?" and accuse God of treating him unfairly. He just got up, brushed himself off, and went on as if nothing had happened.

It took some time to complete the negotiations between families and plan the wedding and the feast. At the appropriate time, Samson went back to Timnath to claim his bride. When he approached the vineyards, he saw the familiar carcass of the lion. Scavengers had picked it clean and only a few tufts of hair and fur remained on the bones. But when he came abreast of it, he was amazed to see that a swarm of bees had filled the lion's chest cavity with a huge honeycomb. He broke off a generous portion of the comb and enjoyed it as he continued on the journey. He had not told his parents about the lion's attack, but he surely did share with them the sweetness of the honey.

If you hear anyone say that answering the call of God will be like tiptoeing through the tulips, they are greatly mistaken. There are adversaries that roar and pounce out of nowhere, right in the vineyard of the Lord. Trials will severely test your strength, faith, and determination. There is no such thing as an untested life in the kingdom of God.

But it is true that when you are willing to fight and determined to survive the attack, God infuses you with a surge of strength so you are able to overcome the enemy. Instead of displaying your wounds, your scars, and your fears, start looking for the honey. Look for the carcasses of old enemies you conquered. Think of how God brought you through by His strong right arm. Think about His love and enablement. Rehearse the story of the victories He has given you.

You might not find the honey right away, but eventually you will, and the taste of it will be so sweet that you can't resist sharing it with someone else.

Samson was not a superhero. He didn't stride from one victory to the next. All of his days were not good ones. It seems as if he swung back and forth like a pendulum between triumph and tragedy. His parents had had such high hopes for their only son, but that son became their most painful heartache. He had a bad habit of yielding to temptation.

One day Samson was burning the enemies' fields and mowing the owners down right and left, but the next he was revealing the secret source of his strength to a nagging, treacherous woman. One day he was slaying a thousand of God's enemies with the jawbone of a donkey, but the next he was having his eyes put out and being forced to grind at the mill in the prison house. His birth had been a miracle, but his foolhardiness constantly endangered the life God had given him.

Our imperfections may be barely a blip on the radar compared to Samson's, but my point is that even though we're not perfect, God still cares and He does not give up. He doesn't want us to either. When Samson thought he would be forced to grind at the mill until his life, like the grain, had been ground up and poured down the chute, God gave him the greatest victory of his lifetime.

God's perfection makes up for our imperfections. All of our victories come from Him and because of Him. When we find the honey, He does not shoo us away from it and claim it for Himself. Instead, He says, "Go ahead and enjoy it!" Like the psalmist we can say, "How sweet are thy words unto my taste! yea, sweeter than honey to my mouth!" (Psalm 119:103).

One time King Saul and the Israelite army were up against it, so the king called a fast in an attempt to curry God's favor. One of the main difficulties was that, in an army of six hundred, the only ones

who had a sword and a spear were Saul and his son
Jonathan. For a long time all of Israel had had to
take their plowshares and mattocks to the Philistine
blacksmiths and pay exorbitant prices to get them
sharpened. Saul was tired of it, so he assembled his
army in Gibeah, his childhood home and now his
royal headquarters.

Without telling his father what he planned to do,
Jonathan beckoned his armor-bearer to follow him.
"Let's go up to the Philistine outpost in Michmash
and see if the Lord will act on our behalf." Michmash
was a little to the northeast of Gibeah, situated in a
pass guarded by two steep cliffs, with the outpost
at the top of one of the cliffs. Jonathan said, "Let's
show ourselves to the Philistines. If they say, 'Come
up to us,' that will be our sign that God will give
us victory." They stepped out from cover and the
Philistines spotted them immediately. They yelled,
"Hey, look! Two Israelite fools just crawled out
from under their rock! Come up here you cowards
and we'll teach you to be afraid of us!"

Jonathan and his armor-bearer found finger holds
and toe holds to scale the cliff. When they reached
the top, they waded into the Philistines so fero-
ciously that twenty of them fell. Israelite deserters
who had hidden in the hills of Ephraim heard the
noise and joined in the fray. The Philistines turned
and ran.

Saul heard the ruckus too. He knew their lack of
weapons could cause them to lose to the well-armed

Philistines, but the outbreak of conflict could be their springboard to victory. He bellowed, "No one is to eat anything this day or you will suffer a curse!" They joined in the chase, seizing Philistine swords along the way.

Jonathan did not hear that food was forbidden; he had been in the thick of battle when his father issued the order. When the army entered a wood, he spotted a honeycomb on the ground, scooped some up, and enjoyed it. Others saw him eating it and their mouths watered. Finally someone warned, "Your father put a curse on anyone who eats anything this day." Jonathan replied, "That's ridiculous. Look how this honey has refreshed me. If all of us would eat today, just think how many more Philistines we could slay. Here . . . why don't you try some?" But no one would because they were afraid of Saul.

Honey is so sweet that we, like Jonathan, want to share it with others. We want to "publish with the voice of thanksgiving, and tell of all thy wondrous works" (Psalm 26:7).

Instead of displaying your wounds, your scars, your fears, and your struggles to survive, share the honey of your victory with others, and your success will strengthen them. The first time you find honey, the burst of flavor is so exhilarating that you want to find more. You begin to view the kingdom with a positive outlook. You know there will be battles and struggles, but tasting the victory is worth the struggle to overcome, and it gives you the strength to do it.

Your list of victories is different from mine. One reason is that our adversary makes it his business to know what troubles us the most. He knows our areas of weakness and attacks wherever he can find a breach. But when you begin to trust in the divine surge of strength, God will help you win the first battle, and many more.

What could you categorize as a victory? Anything you have overcome, whether small or great. Here are some examples:

- Break a bad habit.
- Overcome evil with good.
- Recover from an illness or injury even though the doctor said it was impossible.
- Resist a temptation.
- Do something God asked you to do that you thought was beyond your capability.
- Do unto someone as you would have him do to you instead of what you really felt like doing.
- Teach someone a Bible study, although you thought you couldn't.
- Smile and brighten someone's day even when you feel as if you're under a dark cloud.
- Refuse to retaliate even when someone does you wrong. Instead, forgive.

- Give—money, time, effort, food, or goods—to someone, even though you wanted to hoard them for yourself. Maybe God gave you more than enough sweetness so you could share with someone else.

Your list could be endless. All the problems you have conquered are like moldering carcasses strewn among the underbrush, behind boulders, or in the ditch along your path through the kingdom. It would seem that nothing good could be found in any of those carcasses. But that's the best place to find some honey!

Here are four guidelines about honey:

1. It is easy to get lopsided in our view of life in the kingdom. We need to learn to keep a good balance, accepting the bad but always looking and waiting for the good we know will come. God tells His children to be content and to rejoice, but sometimes that has to be done with gritted teeth because things look so bad. Complaining about it only leaves a bad taste in our mouth. Good times are wonderful, but in the back of our mind we know that trouble of some kind could be waiting in a tree to leap down on us when we least expect it. Job asked, "Shall we accept good from God, and not trouble?" (Job 2:10, NIV). On the other hand, if you never have any adversity, there

would be no possibility of overcoming it. Then you would miss finding the sweetest honey of all.

2. Sometimes people put you on a guilt trip for savoring your honey. They won't eat any even if you offer them some. They like the perceived deprivation and hardship. They miss the point if they haven't ever found out that serving God is sweet. However, when you find honey, eat it in moderation — gorging yourself will ruin the treat. "Do you like honey? Don't eat too much of it, or it will make you sick!" (Proverbs 25:16, *The Living Bible*). Jonathan didn't stand there and eat all the honey, but he did eat enough to give him the energy for the next battle, and it brightened his outlook.

3. Share your honey. Letting someone help you eat it does not diminish your enjoyment; instead, the sharing heightens it. Next time you find some, say to a passerby, "Taste and see that the LORD is good" (Psalm 34:8). Ironically, David wrote Psalm 34 when he was in danger of losing his life. His own king was chasing him from Dan to Beersheba, and when he went to live in the land of the Philistines, they turned on him too. Still, he could say, "I will bless the LORD at all times," both good and bad. Maybe the next time you feel cornered by enemies, a friend will stop

and share their honey with you. It will give you strength to fight again.

4. You don't have to be perfect in order to taste the honey of victory. Ideally, doing the first guideline would keep you on an even keel: calm and consistent. But sometimes you might succumb to the Samson Syndrome. A "syndrome" is a distinctive or characteristic pattern of behavior, and that's what Samson had: a distinctive pattern of swinging back and forth from victory to defeat. Reality says that you won't win every battle, but even if you lose some, you can still win some! Samson made it to the list of heroes in Hebrews 11. All of those heroes were flawed in some way, but with God's help they won.

Chapter 13

In the Morning It Was Leah

*A*nd Jacob served seven years for Rachel; and *they seemed unto him but a few days, for the love he had to her. And Jacob said unto Laban, Give me my wife, for my days are fulfilled that I may go in unto her. And Laban gathered together all the men of the place, and made a feast. And it came to pass in the evening, that he took Leah his daughter, and brought her to him; and he went in unto her.*

. . . And it came to pass, that in the morning, behold, it was Leah: and he said to Laban, What is this thou hast done unto me? did not I serve with thee for Rachel? wherefore then hast thou beguiled me? (Genesis 29:20-25).

This must be one of the most baffling stories in the Bible. It is the story of Jacob, who worked seven years for his uncle Laban to earn the right to marry his daughter, the beautiful Rachel. After the couple's first night together, Jacob woke up and reached for the woman lying beside him—but instead of his beloved Rachel, it was Leah, her weak-eyed older sister. He had married the wrong woman!

This was unheard of. If, as Laban said, he was following the custom of Padan-aram that none of a man's daughters could marry before the eldest did, Jacob had never heard of it. He was dumbfounded and very, very angry.

What can we learn from Jacob's bewildering experience? Is it that we should advise all grooms to lift their bride's veil before spending the night with her so they don't end up with the wrong woman? I don't think so.

Maybe the lesson for us is a little more subtle. Since the Old Testament is filled with types and shadows, perhaps this "working for Laban to get Rachel but waking up with Leah" is a concept that can speak to us in the twenty-first century.

To arrive at a better understanding, let's go back to where the story began in the land of Canaan.

It was the custom of Jacob's people that the first-born son should receive the birthright and a special blessing from his father. This was a big deal. The birthright meant that the firstborn son would receive a double portion of his father's assets when his father died. As the expected successor, the son enjoyed a position of great respect because everyone knew he was the future leader of the family. The blessing went hand in hand with the birthright. The patri-arch bestowed upon his eldest son a blessing that contained monetary, social, and spiritual favor and leadership.

Jacob and Esau were twins, but the birthright and blessing were Esau's because he was the firstborn. But Esau was a profane man (Hebrews 12:16); he "despised" his birthright. He showed his contempt for his father when he sold the birthright to his brother for a meal of bread and pottage of lentils to appease his hunger. I suppose he thought nothing of this transaction because he was sure it would not count. He knew that as the firstborn he would get the birthright and the blessing in the end.

By the time the twins were forty years old, Isaac's eyes were growing dim and he knew it was time to bestow the blessing on his firstborn. He sent Esau, his favorite son and a mighty hunter, out to kill a deer and cook a tasty pot of venison stew. After Isaac had savored the stew, he planned to bestow the blessing.

But while Esau was out in the fields, Rebekah conspired with Jacob to steal the blessing. She created a stew of goat meat that tasted like venison. She helped Jacob fasten goat skins to his arms and neck to make them feel hairy like his brother's. The finishing touch was to dress Jacob in Esau's clothes so he would smell like the fields.

Jacob took the steaming bowl of stew into his father's tent. Isaac turned his head toward his son, but all he could see was a shadowy form. At first Isaac wasn't sure the right son had entered the tent because, for one thing, he couldn't believe Esau had bagged a deer and cooked the venison in such a short time. Also, the young man's voice wasn't as deep and gruff as Esau's. But after Isaac felt of the hairy goat skins and smelled the outdoorsy aroma of Esau's clothes, he ate the spicy stew and washed it down with wine. When he was ready, he blessed his son with the promise of bumper crops, leadership over surrounding nations, and the respect of his brothers and kin.

Not long after Jacob had left his father's tent, Esau entered it with a bowl of genuine venison stew. "Here you are, Father. I've brought your favorite meal you asked for." Bewildered, Isaac said, "Who are *you*?" Esau must have thought his father was daft because just a couple of hours ago Isaac had sent him out to kill a deer and bring him the stew. "Father, who else could I be but Esau, your firstborn? I've done what you asked, and here's the stew." "But . . . but I thought the man who just came in here was Esau. I already ate the stew he brought and gave him the blessing."

Outside, Jacob quaked in his boots when he heard the roar that came from inside Isaac's tent. The roar changed to gut-wrenching sobs as Esau tried to persuade Isaac to change his mind and give him the blessing after all. "I'm sorry, son, I already gave your brother the blessing and it can't be undone." The flow of tears stopped and Esau said in a menacing voice, "This is the second time that weasel has tricked me! First he stole my birthright, and now he's stolen my blessing. When you and Mother named him Jacob, you chose rightly. He's a cheater and . . ."

Esau caught himself before he said, ". . . and I'm going to kill him!" But he knew that would be unwise. Instead, he thought, "I'll wait until after Father is gone, then I'll kill that conniver!"

Jacob and Rebekah looked at each other, eyes wide with fear. Rebekah was well aware of her eldest's penchant for violence. "Quickly, son, you'll have to leave. Your brother's mad enough to kill you." They packed a bundle for Jacob to take with him. "I want you to go to Haran, my hometown. I'm sure my brother Laban will take you in. It's far enough away that you'll be safe from Esau."

Jacob traveled from Beersheba, west of the Dead Sea, all the way to the east of the Euphrates River. When he finally approached what he thought was the general area of Haran, he came across some shepherds waiting until all the flocks had gathered before they removed the heavy stone from the mouth of the well and watered the sheep. They invited Jacob to sit with them. He asked the shepherds where they were from, and they replied "Haran." Jacob asked if they knew Laban, and the shepherds said yes. They all looked up to see a young woman approaching at the head of a large flock of sheep. "You're in luck," said one of the shepherds. "There's his daughter Rachel."

As the woman drew nearer, Jacob saw she was well-favored, and her smile dazzled his eyes. She was the loveliest thing he had ever seen! Even though it wasn't yet time to water the sheep, and even though it usually took several men to move the stone, Jacob strode over to it and muscled the cover off the well. He helped Rachel water her flock while he introduced himself as her aunt Rebekah's son. He leaned close to the woman and kissed her cheek, fighting tears at the thought that he was now safe from the wrath of his brother, and already thinking how lucky he was to find this beautiful woman among his kinfolk.

Rachel ran home to tell her father the news of his nephew's arrival, and the whole family gathered to welcome Jacob. He saw that Rachel had a sister, Leah, who wasn't nearly as pretty; in his eyes she looked stolid and frumpy, unlike her vibrant, lissome sister whose glances contained so much promise. During his first few weeks with Laban's family, Leah always seemed to be hanging around when all Jacob wanted to do was spend time with Rachel. Irritated, Jacob saw Leah as clingy and with a tendency to nag, and he hated that. She always complained of being worn out with all the tasks she had to do, and some of those tasks were ones her sister had ignored. Jacob would never think of pursuing a woman like Leah.

He had enjoyed his uncle's hospitality for a month before he broached the subject of asking for

Rachel's hand in marriage. Laban thought it over before he said, "You don't have any property. What will you do to earn the bride price?" Without hesitation, Jacob replied, "I'll work for you for seven years for your younger daughter Rachel." "Well, I'd rather have you for a son-in-law than most of the others who've shown interest in her. It's a deal."

The seven years seemed to fast forward until it was finally time for Jacob to receive his reward after all the hard work. It seems strange to our western thinking, but the feast Laban provided was for men only. On the last day of the feast, when the sun had slipped below the horizon, he brought a heavily veiled woman to Jacob, and the bridegroom took her to his tent and joyfully made her his wife.

But in the morning when he woke up beside his beloved, it wasn't Rachel—it was Leah! Jacob jumped out of bed as if he'd been stung by a scorpion. His rage blinded him to the stricken look in his bride's eyes. He blamed her for the deception, but then he realized this was his father-in-law's doing. He threw on some clothes and stalked out of the tent to find Laban.

The wily father-in-law didn't look especially perturbed when confronted by his irate son-in-law who yelled, "Why did you do this to me? We agreed that I would work seven years for *Rachel,* not for *Leah!*" His wrath and indignation blotted out the memory of how he had deceived his father and tricked his brother.

"Oh, did I forget to tell you about our custom here in Haran that it is impossible to give any of my daughters in marriage until the firstborn daughter has been wed? Since you were the only one asking to wed one of my daughters, I just knew you wouldn't mind having Leah too." "I see now," sneered Jacob, "it was a setup. From the beginning you planned to trick me." He itched to grab Laban by the throat.

Laban said, "Look, I'll tell you what I'll do. Stay with Leah for a week, then I'll give you Rachel. But your seven years of labor will count for Leah's bride price . . ." Jacob snorted. "You must work another seven years for Rachel." Laban paused and a serious look came into his eyes. "Leah's a good girl and will be a good wife." Jacob sullenly did as Laban asked, but he couldn't wait until another week had gone by and he could finally claim the bride he wanted.

It wasn't easy being married to these two sisters. His thoughts were only for Rachel and he ignored Leah, who continued doggedly with her work. But as the months passed and Rachel failed to conceive a child, he begrudgingly turned to Leah, who conceived right away. In fact, while Rachel remained barren, Leah gave Jacob four sons in quick succession. As each son was born, Leah hoped for Jacob's love, but she was painfully aware that he continued to withhold it. She felt unwanted, unloved, and used. What more did she have to do to win a little of his affection?

After the fourth son was born, it was a long time before Jacob again visited Leah's tent. Finally she couldn't bear the thought that she would never receive any more of his attention, so she bargained with Rachel in order to spend some time with Jacob. After only one night together, Leah conceived a fifth son and then shortly afterward, a sixth son. She thought, "Now Jacob will stay in my tent because I've given him something Rachel couldn't give." She longed to arouse the same glint in Jacob's eyes as when he looked at Rachel.

Like Jacob, we too have dreams and plans that we're willing to work for. Rachel represents everything beautiful we dream of having or accomplishing. She represents a shining future far beyond our expectations, and our heart leaps for joy at the thought of her. She is easy to love. We look forward to getting rewarded for our efforts. The time we spend laboring to achieve the dream seems to fly by. We expect to reach all of our goals without strife and struggle.

Conversely, Leah represents disappointment and pain. She represents our shattered dreams and broken heart. It seems that our time and effort have been wasted when all we get is Leah. She is always hounding us for attention; living with her is frustrating and depressing and sometimes disgusting. She wears us out.

How many times have you thought you were going to get Rachel, the love of your life, but when the morning light came, there was weak-eyed Leah staring back at you? Every dream, every plan, every promise is shipwrecked on the rocks of lies and deception. All of that work for Rachel has been wasted. Living with Leah could represent some sort of addiction to drugs or alcohol, divorce, abusive relationships, betrayal, economic reverses, or the result of bad choices or poor decisions. You never started out to marry anything like that, but you woke up one morning, and there it was. It attaches itself to you and though you despise it, it lingers there in the shadows of your life. It becomes an inseparable part of who you are, and you hate it.

How can this possibly happen? It is a setup, a trick of Satan as old as time itself. He tricked the first people on earth and since it worked so well, he's been doing it ever since. The first thing he sends is hidden beneath a beautiful veil, so you don't recognize it for what it is. You fall in love at first sight. You get intoxicated with the promise of something beautiful, and then in the morning there is the Leah of heartache, shattered dreams, and a broken heart.

You never asked for so many of life's problems and disappointments, but they showed up anyway, uninvited. And they won't go away.

What can you do? The answer is nothing. You can't rewrite your history or undo what has been done.

But there is a ray of hope. The reality is that Leah gave Jacob six sons while Rachel gave him only two, the much-loved Joseph and the pride of his old age, Benjamin. But among Leah's sons was Judah, the son of praise.

Looking back at my own life, I see all my Leahs: disappointment, hurt, pain, aborted dreams, broken hearts, wasted time, frustration, shattered expectations, cancelled plans, empty promises, false hope, trickery, betrayal, lies, weariness, and sometimes disgust. Leah exposed my weaknesses and broke my heart. But she is what brought me closer to the Lord; because of her, I prayed and sought Him. Satan meant all of this for evil, but God meant it for good. (See Romans 8:28.) Leah showed me how fickle and deceiving life can be and how much I need the Holy Spirit.

You may dream about Rachel in the night, but how will it be when the morning comes? The truth is that more encounters with Jesus are brought about by Leah than by Rachel:

- The woman enervated by a twelve-year issue of blood, her Leah, pressed her way to Jesus and was healed.
- The paralytic by the pool who had suffered for thirty-eight years was delivered.
- The widow who wept on the way to her son's funeral received him again to life.
- The disciples' boat was almost swamped by a raging storm but Jesus calmed the storm.

- The wretched woman at the well who had gone through five bad marriages until she gave up and was now living with a man was cleansed and blessed.
- The demoniac howling among the tombs was delivered and given back his sanity.
- The thief on the cross pleaded for mercy and received the gift of forgiveness.

When we begin to understand this, our perception of Leah changes as Jacob's perception finally did. He mourned for Rachel after she died in childbirth on the long way home from Padan-aram. He had hoped to reach Bethlehem before her time came, but it wasn't to be. Smitten with grief, there was nothing else to do but bury her near to where she had died.

In the ensuing years as his frozen emotions thawed, life with Leah mellowed Jacob in tiny increments. As he softened toward this wife whom he had once despised, he began to appreciate her. She had come in a plain brown wrapper, but as he peeled away the layers he discovered the treasures inside.

He began to see her plodding as dependability and her eternal hoping for his love as faithfulness. What he had thought was clinginess he now perceived as cleaving unto him. He had once hated her nagging voice, but now he realized that all along she had been trying to get him to do right,

especially in dealing with their unruly and sometimes violent sons. And he now saw in Leah's
tender eyes a steady look of love.

Whereas Rachel had flown off the handle in a
crisis, Leah was even-tempered. Rachel had been a
taker; Leah was a giver. Rachel was petulant when
she didn't get her way immediately; Leah was calm
and resigned to her lot. Wherever Rachel had gone,
the emotional atmosphere had crackled, but Leah's
aura exuded peace and comfort. Leah's managerial
and cooking skills far outranked Rachel's; Jacob
saw that the efficient running of their household
was all due to Leah. Startled, Jacob came across a
truth that had been hidden from him: most of the
sisterly conflict had originated from Rachel, not
Leah. Rachel envied Leah and was jealous of her
ability to produce sons. She had declared, "I have
had a great struggle with my sister" (Genesis 30:8).

Most important, Leah was the mother of Judah,
the son of praise. As Jacob lay on his deathbed, he
bestowed a prophecy on each of his sons (Genesis
49). He realized that without Leah his dreams of
founding a nation would never have come to frui-
tion. And Judah's lineage would include a coming
Messiah who would have an eternal reign.

Just before Jacob died, he commanded his sons
to inter him in Machpelah, the traditional burying
place of Jacob's family. He wanted to "sleep" forever
beside Leah. He did not even mention Rachel.

After all the glitz of your desire for Rachel has dissipated and your mourning at her passing is gone, you will finally realize how good it has been to be in Leah's hands. Rachel was exciting, but she loved herself more than she loved you. Leah has always had only you in mind. She wants the best for you. And even though you were hurting after you woke up with her beside you that morning and didn't appreciate her and even despised her at times, after Rachel was gone you began to realize how good Leah has been for you and to you. She has helped you grow as a person and as a Christian. She has drawn you closer to your Savior.

LaVergne, TN USA
18 April 2010
179668LV00002B/1/P